In Bohemia

Katie Swenson

In Bohemia

a memoir of love, loss, and kindness

SCHIFFER
PUBLISHING
4880 Lower Valley Road · Atglen, PA 19310

Other Schiffer Books by Katie Swenson:
Design with Love: At Home in America, 978-0-7643-5993-4

Library of Congress Control Number: 2020930549

Creative direction by Takaaki Matsumoto, Matsumoto Incorporated, New York
Jacket and book design by Robin Brunelle, Matsumoto Incorporated, New York
Design supervision by Amy Wilkins, Matsumoto Incorporated, New York
Illustrations by Zoe Miller

Typeset in Manrope and Minion Pro

ISBN: 978-0-7643-5997-2

Printed in China

Published by Schiffer Publishing, Ltd.
4880 Lower Valley Road
Atglen, PA 19310
Phone: (610) 593-1777; Fax: (610) 593-2002
E-mail: Info@schifferbooks.com
Web: www.schifferbooks.com

For our complete selection of fine books on this and related subjects, please visit our website at www.schifferbooks.com. You may also write for a free catalog.

Schiffer Publishing's titles are available at special discounts for bulk purchases for sales promotions or premiums. Special editions, including personalized covers, corporate imprints, and excerpts, can be created in large quantities for special needs. For more information, contact the publisher.

Image credits: the Scarab, home of Katharine Lee Bates: Harry Connolly; the Scarab, circa 1950–1955: photographer unknown, courtesy Wellesley College Archives Image Gallery; the Scarab, 2019: Harry Connolly; plans of the Scarab, recreated from 1907 plan and 2019 plan: Tommy Schaperkotter; Bohemia, 2019: Harry Connolly; Katie Swenson and Tommy Niles, 2016: courtesy the author; Katharine Coman at Wellesley College, 1885: photographer unknown, courtesy Wellesley College Archives Image Gallery; Katharine Lee Bates at the Scarab, circa 1916: photographer unknown, courtesy Wellesley College Archives Image Gallery; page from the journals of Katharine Lee Bates: courtesy Wellesley College Archives Image Gallery

You were, and will always be, mine in love.

Thomas Edward Niles
(May 25, 1960–May 17, 2017)

Contents

This is your assignment.

Feel all the things. Feel the hard things. The inexplicable things, the things that make you disavow humanity's capacity for redemption. Feel all the maddening paradoxes. Feel overwhelmed, crazy. Feel uncertain. Feel angry. Feel afraid. Feel powerless. Feel frozen. And then FOCUS.

Pick up your pen. Pick up your paintbrush. Pick up your damn chin. Put your two calloused hands on the turntables, in the clay, on the strings. Get behind the camera. Look for that pinprick of light. Look for the truth. (Yes, it is a thing—it still exists.)

Focus on that light. Enlarge it. Reveal the fierce urgency of now. Reveal how shattered we are, how capable of being repaired. But don't lament the break. Nothing new would be built if things were never broken. A wise man once said: there's a crack in everything. That's how the light gets in. Get after that light.

This is your assignment.

—Courtney E. Martin and Wendy MacNaughton

In Bohemia

Introduction

When Tommy Niles died suddenly of a heart attack on May 17, 2017, two months before our wedding, the first thing I remember saying at the hospital was, "I am writing his obituary." In fact, writing his obituary became a team effort, but shortly after his funeral service, the words started flowing. I am not sure why writing emerged as my first instinct, but once I started, I could not stop. What follows are those unfiltered emotions.

I wrote my first poem on my iPhone, furiously typing with both thumbs, sitting in my bed at about midnight in a blur of shock and pain, tears streaming down my face. My three girls came into my bed, wanting to comfort me, but I said, no, I had to keep going. I wrote straight through to the end, barely stopping to breathe. When I was done, I sent it in an email to myself, took a sleeping pill, and cuddled with the girls until we fell asleep. When I got up the next morning around 4 a.m., I corrected a typo or two and posted it to Facebook. I had one thought (if you could even call it a thought), and that was expressing my love. It was all I could think about—well, and the complete and utter pain of Tommy being gone.

"Grief is that last act of love," said Sarah, the pastor at Village Church in Wellesley, Massachusetts, while preparing for Tommy's service. In that first year after his death, writing and grieving seemed the same to me. Writing became an unexpected necessity, a way of loving and honoring this man. Writing was the fullest articulation of love that was available to me. I couldn't just love Tommy now in any normal way, so writing was my way of being with him. I got to learn more every day. I got to hear stories, to research. I got to be curious and discover. I got to fall in love with him all over again. The act of writing forced a rigor of thought that organized my mind and allowed me to clear my head, which at the time was fogged with grief. Posting this writing, capturing and sending it out, seemed to allow me to release that memory or train of thought. I was relieved. I felt sane for that moment.

This is a story about love. Primarily, a romance with a magical man at its center—our hero, Thomas Edward Niles, T.E.N. It is an attempt to be fully present in that love, to let it expand and fill us always with joy, to let it be real, to let it be now, to let it be forever. It is a story about grief, longing, belonging, partnership, passion, family, loss, and kindness (always kindness). It is about wanting to understand and explore the essence of love and connection, death and grief, disorientation and survival. This is a story about community, about the friends, neighbors, teachers, children—all the bodyguards—who held us up and watched over me and my girls.

It is a story about home and about the places we create and that create us in turn, about Tommy's and my shared lifelong work designing beautiful spaces—his bag of tools and need to be fixing, building, improving, glorifying every room and structure he entered. It's a story about *our* home—the Scarab, named after the Egyptian symbol for rebirth and creativity and built a hundred years earlier by two courageous women, Katharine Lee Bates and Katharine Coman, the two Katies. Katharine Lee Bates is best known as the author of *America the Beautiful*, and Katharine Coman was a professor of economics at Wellesley College, around the corner from the Scarab. It's about the memory of these women—one famous, one forgotten—whose love story illustrates what love is. And it's a story about Bohemia, the beautiful room on the third floor of the Scarab where Tommy and I lived, where Katharine Coman died, where Katharine Lee Bates mourned, and where I wrote and wrote through that first searing year, held up by their spirits.

I didn't know when I moved in that I would be reborn in love under the wings of the Scarab. That the two Katies' love story would be my love story. Nor could I have ever imagined that their sorrow would merge with my sorrow, their grief would be my grief, and that they would become my spiritual guides. I couldn't have imagined then how this house would widen my world and deepen my relationships, how it would hold me and cradle me, inspire me and heal me.

Reading Bates's love poetry for Coman after her death, I was transfixed by her beautiful poem *In Bohemia: A Corona of Sonnets*, dedicated to Coman, whom she called Joy of Life. A sonnet, from the Italian *sonetto* (little sound, melody, or song), is a fourteen-line poem that follows a strict structure and rhyme scheme. A corona of sonnets is a cycle of seven sonnets connected by theme, in which the first line of each sonnet repeats the last line of the one preceding it, and the last sonnet repeats the first line of the first. *In Bohemia* has seven sets of seven sonnets, or forty-nine total in which the word joy—for her Joy of Life—appears seventy-three times (see the poem on page 203). It is a crowning achievement for her as a poet and an incredible tribute to her love—and the first line of each sonnet forms the chapter titles for this book.

And so, as I sat loving and grieving, watching the changing sky through the tree house windows of Bohemia, I lived and wrote the story of my love and loss.

1

I Give You Joy, My Dearest.

Death Is Done

MAY 31, 2017
We Get to Keep the Gifts He Gave Us

My friend Holly told me this: We get to keep the gifts he gave us.

There is not a single doubt that we mostly just want to keep him. We want to keep everything about him. The neighbors want him to help clean the garage (again) and throw the football with the boys, passing on an emboldening word about the importance of a losing season. The childhood friend wants to keep the only person who has known her her whole life, words rendered unnecessary. We want him to be the consummate host, glasses never empty, plates full, ice plentiful, beer on tap. We want to hear him sing and play the guitar, out of the shower after yoga while the sweat dries, or before dinner to transition the day. I want him to send me a one-word text "tug" to let me know that he feels the pull of me during the day while we're apart. I want his face on the pillow—silent, still sleeper, and to reach out my toes to encircle his.

But we don't get these daily pleasures, these moments of sublime and sweet nowness.

We want him in our futures. We want him tonight before bed, tomorrow for dinner, at our games, at the lake, at the beach, in Idaho, in Iceland scoping out a new hotel. We want him at graduations, at weddings—at *our* wedding, God help us. We want him to help us move, to pay the toll, to send the grades, to answer the phone, to share our successes. We want to attend the opening of the gorgeous, nearly-killed-you renovation of the Narragansett Electric Company in Providence, Rhode Island, tribulation and glory in built form. We want the mentorship, the teaching, the guiding, and encouraging.

I want the grandbabies, our grandbabies. I want those babies to have him, changing the essence of their souls. We don't get this future—once seemingly ordained. We get the memories, the lessons, the photos, the facts of him. We get our love, our heartache, the impossibility, the absolute unreal made real. But, says Holly, we get to keep the gifts he gave us.

He gave me the gift of his full self. He gave me his stories, his history, his people, his loves, his heroes. He gave me his enthusiasm, his happiness, his joy, his words, his writing. He gave me the love that burned for his sons, my daughters, the neighbors' kids, the friends, the nephews and nieces, and just about any dog. He gave me his evolution, his journey, his getting closer to himself. He gave me myself, fully represented in three dimensions or many more.

He reveled in my glory and my imperfection—somehow, miraculously, perfect in his eyes. He gave me the gift of my children—the time and space and support to parent and to love—reborn with fresh eyes in the light of his adoration. He gave me countless dinners, eggs for breakfast, glasses of water; he nourished, cared for, supported, loved, and held. He made a safe haven for us to be bold. At home and in the world, he gave me the fullness of me.

Would I trade the future for these gifts? Luckily, I suppose, he didn't give us the burden of choosing. I fear I would trade the present, would trade anything for that future, perhaps even these lasting gifts. I would seemingly give up any gift for another morning, another song, another walk to the train, one more minute. But he left us this last gift, of not choosing against ourselves, of insisting on the sanctity of his way.

It's a cruel gift, perhaps an impossible one to receive, to honor, and to keep. But he gave so freely and generously that we can only weep in sadness, but with no regret. In memory but not in anger.

We are changed. I am changed. I am more myself for his love. That is the gift he gave me.

JUNE 3, 2017
You Can't Unsee the Kindness of Others

In yoga class this morning, my teacher, Jordan, said, "The universe gives you opportunity after opportunity to learn what you need to learn." In these past few weeks, I am learning about some things I really never knew. I have witnessed, attended, taken action, and hugged others in their moments of loss, but Tommy's death was the first time I had an insider's view into grief and the profound kindness that resonates around it. I won't attempt to speak of the grief, but I will speak about the kindness. Another of my teachers, Tara, said of the funeral service, the wake, the words, the tribute, the hundreds of children and adults at our home, the flowers, cards, lunches, and cut strawberries, "You can't unsee that. You can't unsee the kindness of others once you have seen it."

Tommy had a special kind of kindness, and that has reverberated in people's memories of him, reflections of what made him so special and how he made them feel. People have said that he may have been the most truly selfless person they knew. But now I get to experience that kindness again and again. I get to witness and receive that selflessness in real time, coming from people in every direction. The truth is that we often do unsee the kindness in others, but what would it be like if we didn't? Last week's flowers die, and new ones arrive. Every day, the mailbox is full of handwritten notes. The hugs are soft and long. Tara says, "It's sorta like attending your own funeral, this outpouring of love, but you are there to receive it." I know the lessons to learn are just starting to unfold, but this opportunity to see the kindness in others will make those easier.

JUNE 7, 2017

I Had Found My Tom

Tommy and I had a great love. It felt and looked magical. But I would say it was also hard earned. We had both been married (I for thirteen years, he for twenty-three), each had three children (three girls for me, three boys for him), each divorced. Divorce itself is a trauma. While I was separated, not yet divorced, my heart literally broke. Although I had never had any heart problems, in February 2008, my nurse practitioner said during a standard checkup, "You have a helluva heart murmur! You've never heard that before?" After a diagnosis of severe mitral valve regurgitation, I had open-heart surgery to repair my mitral valve that May.

Lying on the table at Newton-Wellesley Hospital, having an echocardiogram in the middle of the day. I was so tired and it was dark. On the cold table in my flimsy hospital gown, I dozed. I asked the technician if she thought there was a connection between your heart and your "heart." She could see then the condition of my heart, although I would not know until later. She simply said, "Love is a great healer."

I'd long been attentive to the qualities of couples' relationships. I watched, I noticed: The couple in yoga who were often there together, their mats never touching, but also never out of each other's eyesight. The godparents of my youngest daughter, Bliss; their marriage, each their second, became a template for a loving life. And then there were Tom Marvel and his wife, Lucilla. When Tom, an architect in San Juan, Puerto Rico, died in November 2015, I was so sad to hear the news. I had gotten to know Tom and Lucilla over five or six years when my work took me to Puerto Rico. Trained as an architect and community designer, I worked with Enterprise Community Partners, a nonprofit organization dedicated to the mission that all people require housing that is well designed and affordable to them. My work with architects and social activists through Enterprise's Rose Fellowship program has taken me all over the country—in this case, to San Juan and rural communities in Puerto Rico.

Lucilla and Tom were mentors and partners in our work. They had met while at Harvard and Radcliffe and moved to San Juan as a young married couple, raising three sons and contributing their energies to the island. Lucilla became a social planner, and her book *Listen to What They Say* was my introduction to Puerto Rico. Luckily, a few months before Tom's death I had a layover in San Juan and met them for lunch at La Concha, the beautiful hotel Tom's firm renovated. I sent this note to Lucilla on Tom's death: "You may not know that I actually have used you two as an example of a great couple. Maybe in part because I was divorced, I find myself interested in great couples and what makes them work. I hadn't quite realized that I was keeping a list in my head, but it's true. Julie and Hank . . . Angie and Larry . . . Marc and Jonathan . . . Tom and Lucilla . . . noticing what are the qualities of the individuals and the qualities of their relationship. Of course, you can imagine some of the things I am particularly partial to—a deep love for family and a passion for meaningful work, a clear sense of "I" and a deep commitment to "we," a genuine like of each other and appreciable sense of admiration for the other."

I had finally found my Tom. He fit the bill for all those qualities and more. And we both knew how lucky we were. This second time around, we could create the kind of relationship we wanted and needed. We could lead with kindness and be grateful for not only the love and companionship, but also for the help and partnership.

I wish divorce did not have to be so painful. I wish there could be more kindness in it. I wish we could be easier on ourselves and each other. After spending the evening with a friend who is going through a bitter divorce, I keep thinking, what does death teach us about divorce and other disappointments? Perhaps it seems odd to call death a disappointment, but at its core, that is what it is. The thing you want is not. The thing you don't want is. And yet, there is no one to blame; it just is. And it cannot be changed. I am so grateful that Tommy healed me with his kindness. If I can survive this grief, it will be because of his love.

JUNE 8, 2017
Shavasana

"Do your practice, all is coming."

When Tommy and I first started doing yoga together, we used to hold hands in shavasana, corpse pose, my left pinkie and ring finger and his right. We preferred to practice side by side, but since we usually arrived just as class was beginning, sometimes that wasn't possible. He wanted to be on my left, and I developed certain habits around that. After the standing poses, when we would first hit the floor, I'd always turn my head to the left, and he'd turn his to the right. I'd whisper or mouth, "Hey, baby," and he'd whisper back. Even when I went alone, I'd find myself whispering it to him in my mind.

People have asked if—or how—I can still go to yoga. Fact is, you couldn't keep me away. I've been doing yoga since I moved to New York in 1990, and it's been one of the most essential and fulfilling parts of my life to this day. At the wake I told Jordan that I had practiced that morning. I had gone to class with two of my daughters, Sophie and Bliss, to wring out all the sweat, tears, and tension before we greeted hundreds of people. I was so filled with adrenaline that day, I nearly flew through class. Jordan replied simply, "This is what we practice for."

But I also go there to be with Tommy. After some time, we decided not to touch fingers in shavasana—our favorite pose. Shavasana is something to experience alone, and the touch of another—or one's own movement, even a twitch or a breath—disrupts one's ability to fully let go. Tommy loved the way Jordan would talk us through shavasana, the same way he talked his daughter Penelope into relaxing before bedtime. "Feel your pinkie, the whole pinkie," he says, going from one body part to the next, focusing on and then relaxing each part, until he says, "Feel the whole body, the whole body." Tommy told me that in stressful meetings, he would relax by repeating to himself, "Feel the whole body, the whole body." After corpse pose, we would roll to our sides into fetal position, which was also a sort of spooning pose. I'd scoot back a little, for a moment feeling my backside press against him before sitting up, eyes closed, to finish the class.

Yoga is the practice of dying and being reborn, again and again, every day. Perhaps it's no surprise, then, that Tommy died so beautifully. The morning of his death, he wanted to make sure we were side by side. It was a lovely morning in Boston. When the alarm went off at 5:10 a.m., the sky was streaked with pink, and Bohemia was rose colored. Tommy got up to start the coffee and I watched him walk naked across our room. While the water was heating, he came back to bed, wanting to make love. I paused, What's the time? 5:25 a.m. "Always time, baby," and there was. He told me that morning that watching me move through our space made his world shift on its axis, and while he told me how he loved me, I remember consciously thinking that it was I who was watching him move through our space, my world again clicking into alignment.

The 5:45 a.m. class we attended was packed. When we rolled in a few minutes late, being together meant being in the front row, not our ideal, but he was determined we be next to each other. We laid out our mats and had a practice as perfect, in its remarkable ordinariness, as any other.

I heard later that people noticed us that day, right up front and center. But when Tommy took off his glasses for class, he couldn't see a thing more than a foot or two away. I used to tease him that his vision without glasses was about the distance of a nursing baby to a mother's face. When he was in yoga, I don't think he saw anything but me; at least that is the way it felt.

After class, he did his twenty-five push-ups; the wedding was two months away and he was getting ready. He cleaned the blocks, went out to the hall, and changed into dry clothes. I chatted with Tara in the room, in no hurry to leave. We were talking about the wedding. When I got to the hall, he was alone, lying on his back, struggling to breathe, sweating, and saying his hands were tingling. My instinct was to get water and a towel, but Tara immediately called 911. The EMTs paddled and pumped, but after the first shock, when he came to, he was perfectly still. The EMTs moved around him for many more minutes, getting him onto the gurney, but he was still at the center. His breathtakingly handsome face was getting both more angled and softer, like water polishing a stone, but on super-accelerated time.

I didn't know; my mind couldn't even manufacture an outcome of death. Although the seriousness was mounting and I called his sons from the ambulance, the first moment I saw that possibility in my mind was when the EMTs were taking him out of the ambulance; he was so still, and I saw his fingers rolled up in just that way of corpse pose. How long can the brain go without oxygen? I was unable to do the math in my head.

The doctors stood ready as the nurses kept pumping, and I held his feet, shins, and hands and stroked his face and his beautiful shoulders and breastbones. He was warm and still, and his body was its beautiful self. I couldn't take my hands off him, but of course, I never could take my hands off him. He loved nothing more than being touched.

A young woman was still in the studio after class that day. I didn't know her and simply called her my angel, sent to witness his death. She said that after the first shock, he did wake up, called my name, "Katie." "I'm right here with you, baby," I said. How I could be so lucky on that unluckiest of days, I'll never know. I thank God that the people around us knew what to do and did, taking action to try to stop the impossible from happening. They allowed me to just be there with him; my only job was to love him.

I'd never seen death before, but in his case, it looked a lot like the serenity of corpse pose. When I lie in shavasana now, I feel his beautiful, still self, somehow peaceful despite my mounting anguish. I'm still whispering to him in class, "I'm right here with you, baby." But then I roll to the right, rest there a moment, and sit up to begin again.

JUNE 10, 2017
Yellow Clover

As I sit now in this perch, writing love letters, writing eulogies, writing loss and yearning, I don't know how I have come to this place. When I first visited this big, drafty house in 2007, I was ready for my own rebirth, and the story of Katharine Lee Bates drew me in. Our arrival marked the hundred-year anniversary of the house in Wellesley, Massachusetts, built in 1907 by Katharine Lee Bates (1859–1929) and Katharine Coman (1857–1915). Traveling in Egypt while it was under construction, Bates named the house the Scarab after the Egyptian beetle, a sign of rebirth and regeneration, and came home with a decorative scarab that she embedded in the mantelpiece. They had little furniture, and it took them a few years to settle in. It's incredible to think that these professors (women!) had the means to hire an architect to design such a wonderful house.

By the time I arrived, the house had been sitting empty for at least three years and needed major renovations. My mom, the ultimate project-doer and home maker got started before we arrived, painting the girls' rooms—orange for Sophie, light green for Liv, and pink for Bliss; they were ten, seven, and three at the time. We squatted at first, a temporary kitchen in the dining room, a makeshift bath on the second floor. I took on one project at a time—the electrical system and kitchen, then the heating system and insulation, moving room by room, year by year through the house.

My family was close by, my parents living a few miles away and my sister, Chrissie, and her family even closer, but I was new to the neighborhood, a single woman in a community of couples. This house, through the daily tending of it, and these Wellesley professors, through their unique story, became part of my life. Bates wrote to a friend about being a "fringe on the garment of life." She said, "I always thought the fringe had the best of it, and I don't think I mind being not woven in." I loved her attitude, and with each year I got to know both the house and their story better. I met Bates's nephew when he came to town. I found artifacts in the house. I read. But I had no idea that renovating Bohemia, the magical third-floor space that Tommy and I eventually remade, would open up to me the story of Bates and Coman's love and adventurous spirits—and also their grief and loss in the last chapters of their lives.

An English professor at Wellesley College, Bates was interested in American authors and a particular fan of Nathaniel Hawthorne. In her introduction to the 1902 edition of *The House of Seven Gables*, Bates lovingly describes Hawthorne's wife making a workspace for her husband and listening to him read his first verses. It's touching, this intimate view into Hawthorne's domestic life.

Many at Wellesley would have studied Hawthorne, including their colleague Hannah Davidson, who, in 1906, had hired local architect William Brainerd to draw an illustration of what the House of Seven Gables would have looked like had it not been fictional. Bates and Coman subsequently hired Brainerd to design their own house, based in part on Brainerd's renderings of the imaginary House of Seven Gables. I learned this part of the story from Alice Friedman, an architectural historian at Wellesley College. Alice came for dinner and took an interest in the house, later researching and writing a paper called "Hiding in Plain Sight: Life, Love and the Queering of Domesticity in Early Twentieth-Century New England." She calls the house a "poker face," meaning that it presents a normative facade to the suburban context, but that inside, a nontraditional domestic arrangement—love between two intellectual, professional women, a partnership of equals—animated the house.

Alice also found many references in the Scarab to *The House of Seven Gables*—the Delft tiles in the family room, which Bates and Coman named the Haven after the Pyncheon House's parlor in Hawthorne's novel. The third-floor working space, Bohemia, was perhaps partly modeled on Hawthorne's real-life third-floor writing room in his house in Concord, Massachusetts—a place to work above the domestic chaos, a writing space that Bates created for her beloved Coman.

The House of Seven Gables was an interesting choice of inspiration for the Scarab. Hawthorne's novel begins, "Half-way down a bye-street of one of our New England towns stands a rusty wooden house, with seven acutely-peaked gables, facing toward various points of the compass, and a huge clustered chimney in the midst." He continues, "The aspect of the venerable mansion has always affected me like a human countenance, bearing the traces not merely of outward storm and sunshine, but expressive, also, of the long lapse of mortal life, and its accompanying vicissitudes that have passed within." The house is both a character and the setting for the drama.

I grew up knowing about Bates, one of Wellesley's most famous residents, as the writer of the poem "America the Beautiful." But after I bought the house, my friend Robin gave me a biography of Bates called *Dream and Deed: The Story of Katharine Lee Bates*, written by her niece, Dorothy Burgess. Robin lovingly placed sticky tabs on every page the Scarab was mentioned, and this act of kindness invited me to approach this move with more curiosity than dread. I discovered a rich story of Wellesley and the house: birthplace of women's education; canvas for Frederick Law Olmsted Jr.'s landscape architecture and horticulture; a house full of ambitious, radical women, writers, poets, and activists, complete with dinner parties, salons, students, and visiting poets. A screened porch in the woods, a sleeping porch off the bedroom.

Over the years, I would learn more about these two Katies—their trek across the country to Colorado College, where "America the Beautiful" would take form in Bates's head. About Bates's dozens more works of poetry, literary theory, children's literature. About her teaching career, extensive travel and friendships, and robust personality.

I would learn more about Katharine Coman also. Coman graduated with a PhD from the University of Michigan and came to Wellesley College in 1880 as a director of rhetoric. She advanced to professor of history in 1881, but her focus was always on political economy. When history and economics were divided into two departments in 1897, Coman took over the political economy and sociology departments, the most-popular fields of study at Wellesley at the time. She served as dean of the college in 1900 and continued as a professor until 1913. What's more, she was an activist for women's rights, part of the early Settlement House movement, a labor activist, photographer, and clearly a remarkable woman.

Bohemia was designed to be Coman's writing room, a creative space in the trees. She wrote extensively, revising *Industrial History of the United States* and researching and writing *Economic Beginnings of the Far West: How We Won the Land beyond the Mississippi* while battling breast cancer. Having found "a tiny lump" in 1911, Coman had numerous and certainly brutal surgeries, ultimately retreating to Bohemia full time. She died there on January 11, 1915. Bates survived her by fourteen years, moving up to Bohemia herself. She wrote poem after poem about her love and grief and published those poems in *Yellow Clover: A Book of Remembrance*, dedicated to Coman.

Bates never stopped loving and grieving, but her life went on, as life does. She continued teaching at Wellesley College, and the Scarab was full of visiting poets and friends. A classmate of Bates writes in the introduction to *Selected Poems by Katharine Lee Bates*, "Most of the poets welcomed at the college found their way to the Scarab and its poet mistress and formed lasting friendships there. Yeats and Gibson from overseas, and, from nearer home Robert Frost, whom Bates mentored, and Bliss Carman, Lizette Woodworth Reese, Anna Hempstead Branch, Leonard Bacon, and John Neihardt are but a few. Neihardt wrote afterwards that his hour with Miss Bates was worth the long train trip from St. Louis. But the charm of quiet talk with the great-hearted, great-minded occupant of this delightful study, with its friendly firelight playing over cherished books and souvenirs of travel, with the bright-eyed elder sister dropping in for a word of greeting, with Sigurd or his shy successor Hamlet standing up for a caress—ah, who can capture it!"

Bates and Coman had built this house to make their own world, which is to me the highest form of architectural design. Dorothea Lawrence Mann wrote in *Katharine Lee Bates: Professor and Poet*, "The house on Curve Street stood first of all for friendship. It was founded on the wonderful friendship of Miss Bates and Miss Katharine Coman, who was formerly Wellesley's professor of economics and history, that friendship which is commemorated in the most beautiful of Miss Bates's books, her *Yellow Clover*. It was as well the house of other friendships. One always knew welcome there, no matter how loudly the dogs might bark—Sigurd in welcome and Hamlet in fear. The house on Curve Street was such a pleasant place to linger—the book-lined rooms, the study looking out on the 'jungle' where in early summer the laurels bloomed so abundantly, reminiscent of that exquisite lyric, 'I count the years by Junes which flush our laurel.'"

My girls and I embraced that spirit and, over the years, remade the Scarab as welcoming and eclectic, full of friends, guests, and creative energy. When Tommy moved in, it seemed like he brought with him a giant "Welcome to the Scarab" sign. He was totally at ease in this house of women, by women, for women. For a short time, he brought his giant, aging rottweiler, Laila, who sat in the front hall, guarding both entrances, regal and protective. Tommy was like our king, but one who needed no throne. But then, poof. He is gone. A matter of minutes, and no return. And I am here, we are here, we women, in this place that we made our own, this bohemia of our imagination turned into physical form, this Scarab needing yet more rebirth, further regeneration.

JUNE 11, 2017

There Are Words

I am thinking about writing, and words occur nonstop. "There are no words" to describe the sadness, I hear over and over. No one knows what to say. One of my closest friends can talk to me about anything, but because of her proximity she can see so clearly, in detail, the depth of the loss in so many facets that it renders her speechless, still in a state of shock.

Notes, poems, and books arrive, gifts of words and compassion, wisdom, and encouragement. I read and reread the cards, each a gesture of love. I have yet to start on the books; everything is too raw, and reading feels too abstract yet, someone else's experience. All I want is to be present in this moment, loving Tommy.

If grief is that last act of love, writing and grieving have become the same, an unexpected necessity, a way of loving and honoring this man. I am

I GIVE YOU JOY, MY DEAREST. DEATH IS DONE

writing all day in my head. There are so many questions, thoughts, memories causing chaos in my mind, and I find myself working to organize those thoughts into some sort of cohesion. I especially "write" in yoga every day, which may be why so many of my reflections are based there. In yoga, it's freeing to be able to follow the instructions, keep the body in motion, breathe, let my brain rest and my mind wander. It's the place where I can relax best, can be calm and quiet. Unlike in bed, where sadness and anxiety overwhelm me, I can be in that space with Tommy peacefully, loving him and grieving him.

As my mind is chasing memories, images, words, gestures, people, I find myself wanting to hold on, and fear losing Tommy more as each day passes. My friend Brad, play-by-play commentator of my life since the seventh grade, tells me I don't have to remember everything, that he and others can help. But I am plagued by forgetfulness. Which Pearl Jam album was Tommy listening to last week when he picked me up at the airport at midnight, telling me the story of a dark time in the 1990s when music saved his soul? What was that saying he often referenced, the one about "always" and "never"? I can't remember and it torments my mind, too cluttered to let clarity come.

Intimate love is not necessarily to be lived out loud. While Tommy was alive I did not need to reflect so much, and when I did, it was mostly with him. We talked about everything between us, around us. He was a storyteller and would talk about interests, people, and experiences in incredible detail. Now I know how lucky I was that he would tell some of the same stories again and again, adding a new layer of perspective or detail.

How do you love someone who is gone? If it is through memory, then how do you remember? I crave the stories people tell about him, the parts I don't know but that fill out his essence. But I also need to remember in just my most personal way. Some days I have the presence to write down what I am writing in my mind; other days I don't. The stuff I don't write rattles on, incoherent. Writing has become my saving grace, the act of doing it and the fact of it being done, a moment of sanity in the chaos of grief, and perhaps insanity too, a way to talk with Tommy, to continue our unending conversation.

JUNE 12, 2017
Mother's Day

One night last week, a dozen or so friends came for dinner. They brought food and drinks, and it felt so good to sit and talk with people I love. After we said our goodbyes, I went to the kitchen to turn off the lights and discovered that all the food was still out and dishes were everywhere. Panic set in.

Tommy must have been a professional dishwasher in his past life, because, man, could he do the dishes. In everyday life or at a party, we mostly did them together, no matter who cooked that night. There was peacefulness in putting the kitchen back together, another opportunity to bond, working side by side, tending our nest. Sure, one of us would take the job for the other if there was hockey carpool or work to catch up on, but because we'd both been single parents, it was an inexplicable joy to do the dishes together.

That night, I took a breath and finished the dishes, making sure to dry and put everything away just as he did. I headed upstairs, where, it turned out, the girls had not put away the clothes I had washed and folded for them a few days earlier. I heard in my voice a shrillness I had not heard for a while. It was as if I was transported back to my reality for many years: getting three small girls off to school, with the inevitable lateness, forgot something, can we go back, work call starting in five minutes. Panic. I am a single mother again. I apologized to the girls and went to bed, running away from that voice.

I am in a group chat with two beautiful, successful, rock-star moms, both solo heads of households. On Mother's Day weekend, a few days before Tommy's death, I spent the first part of it visiting my oldest daughter in Utah while Tommy was at home with the other two. The women wrote: "That's so wonderful! How incredible you could be there! Here's to the best Moms on the Planet." The other friend replied, "Happy Mother's Day to the smartest, most dedicated, selfless beautiful, badass Mommas I know!" I started to write something back but then deleted it, because it felt wrong. Instead I wrote, "I love you ladies!!!!"

What held me back was the recognition of how incredibly difficult it is to be a solo parent. And how supported I felt at that moment, and how as a result of that partnership, I really was able to be a better parent. For the eight years I was a single mom, I did the best I could, one foot in front of the other. But now I realized what a heavy load that was and how much lighter my life had become. Damn, that is too complicated for a group text.

I absolutely loved being coupled. Having a loving partner is a wonderful way to live, in ways big and small. It's a gift to have the other parent make breakfast, drive to school, or go to the store. It's a gift to have someone tending to some children so you can focus on another. It's a revelation that your children get to see someone adore you, and see you adore that person.

On Mother's Day, back home, I received a card from Tommy, along with beautiful flowers and a steak tip dinner for twelve (including my mother and sister) from him and my brother-in-law. The card read:

May 14, 2017

Dearest Katie,

Our life together has allowed me the gift of witnessing an amazing woman raise three extraordinary, wonderful, beautiful daughters, who, like their mother, will achieve great things and change so many lives and will continue to find success and love at every turn.

I love you,

Tommy

Somehow Tommy saw the job I had done as a single mother not as a cause for distress but as an achievement worthy of admiration. He saw my girls— their capable, resilient, fun-loving, ambitious selves—as a measure of a life well lived. He saw that my career and providing for them was every bit as much a part of parenting as caring for their daily needs. He was especially incredulous that dinner had appeared magically all those years (it really hadn't). Luckily, dinner appeared far more often, and more joyously, when he was on the scene. My return to single-mother status and the loss of Tommy as helpmate are only a fraction of the million ways I miss him.

JUNE 13, 2017
She's Going to Like Me

Tommy told me that the first time he dropped me off at home, the day after we met, he looked at my big, old, shingle-style house and said to himself, "She's going to like me."

Both of us were house and home people. This was true in our choice of careers—he was a builder and real-estate developer, and I am trained as an architect—but we were also both deeply invested in home. Tommy had built his house in Nantucket and rebuilt his family's house. I have renovated every single place I've lived—from college apartment to loft to house—since my freshman year of college. He had serious skills too. A patient carpenter, he could make or fix anything, and he could also design and draw.

Tommy started bringing his tools over to our house, little by little. Fix the storm door, repair the knobs on the stove, get the garage door opener to work, again. I had been renovating the house continuously since I bought it. Before we even moved in, my mom helped me get rid of the old knob-and-tube wiring so I could get homeowners' insurance. I turned to the kitchen first, then bathrooms, painting, heat, insulation, porch. Finally, my neighbors Amy and Stephanie helped me choose the paint colors for the exterior—formerly brown shingles with institutional yellow trim, now graphite shingles with warm, orangey-red window frames and ivory trim. The house was looking pretty good, but there was, and is, a long way to go.

Tommy whistled while he worked; small house projects were like therapy or meditation for him. He installed shelving and redid the closets. He renovated the old storage room as my office, with sliding barn doors and built-in cabinets repurposed from another part of the house.

One night we started talking about the kitchen, lots of plans and ideas brewing. For the short term, we decided to remove a section of the upper cabinets and put up floating shelves. It was Sunday night about 8:30 p.m., and I was leaving on a work trip the next day. He looked at me. "You want to do this now, don't you?" You bet I did. We took down the stretch of upper cabinets, finding instant relief in the new open space. Removing the corner cabinet left a gap. I thought one of the other cabinets we had taken out might fit, and he said that would be too good to be true. Try it. He lifted the cabinet, and it was eerily almost perfect. A little olive oil? Olive oil and a hard shove put the cabinet right into the corner like it belonged there all the time. When I got home two days later, the new floating shelves were up. It was a gift to come home to. They were meant to be temporary, but they are still there. He had patched and painted the wall, but there were a few streaks in the paint. We knew we'd eventually get a fresh coat on the whole kitchen, but of course we haven't.

We worked our way through the house. Some rooms needed more work than others, but over that first year the house became more beautiful and more ours. I love this house, and it loved him. Tending, fixing, making, doing nonstop. More-sophisticated tools arrived, and he started to set up a proper workstation in the garage.

His clothes started to appear in the closet, but it wasn't until we were engaged that he would move in officially. We decided to move to the third floor, Bohemia, reconfiguring the second floor to make a bedroom for the boys, giving Liv what was formerly the master with bath, and moving Sophie, soon off to college, into the small bedroom, formerly my office. Bliss got Liv's old room with the great closet.

We thought the Bohemia renovation would be the first of many projects together. I drew, we discussed. We planned and redrew.

His friend Fernando sent work crews from Rhode Island. Tommy had gone to college at the University of Rhode Island and had lots of friends and colleagues there. His company was renovating one of the glorious Providence electric plants when he died. We would often have six to eight men working on a Saturday, their day off, especially during the finish phase. At 9:15 a.m. we'd call them down for a hearty breakfast, family style. Tommy would make eggs and bacon and we'd prepare a feast. I baked a lot those months, pumpkin bread and chocolate cake. The space started to take shape, and it was glorious—think New York loft surrounded by trees. We took down the dropped ceiling to reveal the Scarab's roofline, like the Egyptian beetle's wings opening. In winter, the sky, light, and snow are mesmerizing, and as spring comes, the room starts to feel like a screened porch, a tree house, surrounded by greenery and breezes.

We moved into the space in January and lived there together, somehow magically in flow. He liked to sit on the couch with his laptop or guitar. I liked to sit at the big table with my computer or drawing board. We loved being in the space together, whether we were working or just hanging out. And now, I don't want to leave this space too often or for too long. It's calming, it's beautiful, it's him, it's us. I know the world is out there, but right now, my world is here.

JUNE 14, 2017

The Thinking Cup

Torrential tears today. Perhaps a big mistake, but at 4 a.m. I was up and trying to sort through thousands of photos. I checked a date on our shared calendar and saw that Tommy had added these notes:

> February 1, 2015: Katie writes an email
>
> March 8, 2015: Piano recital at the Gardner
>
> March 8, 2015: Intercepted! Dammit!
>
> March 11, 2015: Tommy Niles—Bocado
>
> March 12, 2015, 9:30 a.m.: Wait whuuu? Coffee
>
> March 12, 2015, 5:00 p.m.: 1st commute (happy couple)
>
> March 20, 2015, 7:11 p.m.: American Airlines, 1st kiss
>
> (A few more X-rated "firsts" followed.)

Tommy's college friend, whom I knew from yoga class, introduced us by email the winter before we met, in 2014, when Tommy was newly separated. I was at a hockey tournament in New Hampshire with Bliss that weekend. We traded a few emails, but then he wrote back, "I am not ready to meet you yet." For me, this was a no-harm, no-foul situation. I knew little about him aside from a tiny LinkedIn photo and brief bio. On his side, he was in the throes of separated life, with all of its chaos. His friend had been talking me up for months, so an idea about me was already forming. He was too much in the swirl, too broken, too overwhelmed to meet me.

The following winter it snowed more than 100 inches in Boston. The commuter train was constantly delayed, and I spent a lot of time working from home, dueling with ice dams, a broken boiler, and endless piles of snow. It must have been February 1 (says Tommy's note) when I was home, literally cleaning out my email, as one does only when housebound. I came across our email exchange from the previous winter. I wish I could find it now, but I remember thinking how extraordinary it was. Tommy was a great writer, I would learn later, but for now I was intrigued by his language and tone. I remember that he had seen a snowy owl that morning. Without thinking twice, I replied to the year-old email chain, something along the lines of "Hey, how are you? I was just cleaning out my email and came across this message. Girls are great and all's well here. Eternal love remains elusive—Katie."

I guess this time he wasn't going to miss the opportunity. I am pretty sure his response included both "Do you need me to shovel your driveway?" and "Can I drive you to the airport?" Already the caretaker. From there we kept in loose touch, with a few missed opportunities to meet. Finally, we met at a restaurant on March 11, 2015. This year, on March 11, 2017, he wrote to me:

> Dear Katie,
>
> March 11, 2015 was an incredibly memorable and amazing day in my life. In our lives. It led to many of the happiest days of my life, and this wonderful world that we live in together. I am so excited to see what tomorrow brings! I love you.
>
> Tommy

It was that big a day. I had been in New York and took the 4 p.m. Acela home. I went straight from the station to the restaurant, wearing my work clothes and feeling a little dorky, not quite a date outfit. When I walked into the restaurant and scanned the bar, he caught my eye. The tiny LinkedIn photo sort of resembled him. When I saw him, I thought to myself, "You didn't tell me you were my guy." We had a wonderful time, lots of laughter; he walked me to my car and gave me the most awkward of pecks on the cheek. There was a text from him before I got home, just a half mile away. In two days, I would be going away for a week, and later that night I asked him to have coffee with me the following day.

We met at the Thinking Cup on Newbury, near my office. He was there first, nervous, not knowing what was on my mind. He called it the "Wait whuuuu? coffee." The "Is this what I think it is?" coffee. I thought to myself, I think I have just met "my guy," but I really want to know before I head out of town. Later that day he picked me up at my office (happy couple) and we drove home together. I don't think either of us ever looked back.

My coworkers Nella and Kate were on the same flight home the following Friday, but I was off the plane first. When they got to baggage claim, they saw us kissing. Who the heck is that? I'm not sure how I'll resume my traveling life. Of the four or five dozen trips I had taken for work since we met, there were only one or two times that he didn't pick me up or drop me off at the airport or train station.

Monday night before he died, my plane back from a day trip to New York was delayed. The Celtics were on, so staying up late wasn't so bad, but by the time I landed at Logan it was after midnight. The airport was nearly empty, but as I walked through the security doors, there he was.

JUNE 15, 2017
Reiki

Dear Jeannie,

I'm going to try to describe my experience this morning on the Reiki table. First, I trusted you completely—an enormous gift. I didn't have any preconceived notions about what we would be doing, and it felt good to just show up and accept your invitation.

As you started at my feet and ankles, I could immediately feel a mounting distress. I loved Tommy's body, every part of it and especially his feet and ankles. I remember being new lovers and kissing his toes and his feet. He had beautiful feet. Thinking about his feet now swells my heart, and I feel like I am falling more in love with him every minute. It feels like the opposite should be true, but I cannot get away from this vertiginous feeling of falling in love—the instability of it, the thrill, eerily similar to this feeling I have now, whether that's called love or grief.

After you left my feet, they felt pinned, heavy, anchored. As you worked your way along my body, I started to feel like I was in this in-between space—between living and dying, I suppose. It was almost as if I was experiencing what he may have felt as his body became gradually immovable. I had held his feet, stroking his ankles, pressing his toes in my hands. I moved all around his body, wanting him to feel me, to know I was there. How long did he feel me? Was it a few minutes or the hour? As his heart stopped working, did he have feeling in his body? Your hands hovered over me. My whole body felt leaden, and I had a mounting tension in my head, both physical and mental. Did his mind keep working while his heart was stopping, and if so, what did he feel, think, or sense?

For minutes on end I thought maybe I was he and you were me. I was in that experience of my body becoming still and you were laying on your hands, as I had for him. But then it became less clear, maybe he and I were the same body; he was me. Could he possibly be in me? I want that so badly. I want to be able to see how he saw, to think how he thought, to remember how he remembered. I wished he could be reborn in my body, live in me.

As I lay there, you said to move my fingers and toes. I could start to move my fingers, but my toes and feet would not respond. His toes did not come back alive in my hands. I tried and tried to stroke the life and blood back into them, but they were still. They stayed smooth and beloved, soft, and beautiful, but they wouldn't move. I'm sure the doctors and nurses thought I was crazy, but I kissed the soles of his feet. I pressed his shins, his thighs, his hands. I laid my head on his chest and squeezed his shoulders. I kissed his face and stroked his hair. How was it possible that this beautiful body, this man I love, could be so still, could not be waking up?

Now I lay unmoving on the Reiki table, inhabiting this in-between space with him, wanting to be anywhere where he was. I knew I had to get out, to leave him, but my feet and toes would not move, so I finally turned over on my side, back to that fetal position, that place of all things sad and happy, all things asleep and awakening. I miss him so much I can't stand it—more every day, it seems, rather than less.

Love,
Katie

JUNE 16, 2017
Flag Folding

In the first month of our relationship, Tommy and I went to a gala for the Sandra Feinstein-Gamm Theater in Providence, Rhode Island. As we drove south, the stories started to flow, my first real introduction to his life and work in Rhode Island. We pulled up to the historic Pawtucket Armory, built in 1895, red brick, granite, and limestone with a Richardsonian Romanesque entry. While the party was underway in the large drill room, we snuck around the building to investigate, from the round corner Officer's office to the rec room in the basement. Tommy recounted stories of his life in that building during his time in the ROTC and the United States Army in the mid-1980s.

I didn't know what to think about his military service at first. A self-described liberal, I went to the University of California, Berkeley, where I learned how to protest in the streets of San Francisco. I am sure that if Tommy and I had met in the 1980s, it would have been nearly impossible to connect. He was eight years older than I, but we would also have been separated by geography, perspective, and politics.

Learning about his years in the military was a fascinating glimpse into a world I didn't know. He talked about the army the way he talked about football, from the inside as a lived experience, not as a fan or from a political perspective. He joined the ROTC at first for beer money, I think. On a full scholarship at the University of Rhode Island, he was paid $150 per month for being in the ROTC. After he graduated, he was commissioned in the US Army in 1983 as a second lieutenant, serving as company commander in the National Guard, retiring in 1990 as a captain.

He had amassed quite a stack of awards. It seems that everything he did, he did well:

- Army ROTC Scholarship Award for meritorious record in academic and military science studies, having demonstrated exceptional leadership potential
- 1982 Scholarship of American Military Engineers Award in recognition of maintaining high moral and citizenship values

- 1983 ROTC Distinguished Military Graduate and Distinguished Military Student Awards
- 1988 Rhode Island Army National Guard, Outstanding Achievement Award
- 1990 Meritorious Service Medal as company commander for Captain Thomas E. Niles

We hadn't yet found all this documentation as we were planning his memorial service. He'd tell the occasional story about his military service but never talked about his accomplishments. The medals and awards were tucked away in a briefcase on a shelf in the garage. But we knew he would have wanted a proper flag-folding ceremony. Joe Brooks, his friend from URI, made calls to the local command, and we prepared the paperwork to secure the National Guard.

The Village Church had the perfect setting, out front, for the ceremony. There was no one in the church who hadn't cried during the service, not one who could accept the unfairness of this loss. But when the bugle sounded there was silence. This man, our man! We stood and watched as he was honored, the flag him, he the flag, as he was folded once, twice, again and again, so neatly, so squarely, into a perfect recognizable package and handed, complete, to his son.

JUNE 17, 2017
I Got Enough

"I got enough," Tommy would say about his father's death. Tommy's father died when he was twelve. He was diagnosed with lung cancer that winter, underwent surgery that seemed to work, but then took a turn for the worse and died late spring. Somehow, over time, Tommy took this loss in stride. "I got enough," he would say. "He gave me enough."

I'm not sure we could have ever had enough of Tommy Niles. But on Father's Day weekend, especially, I hope and pray that someday his children and my children, his family and friends, will feel that way. Lives will go on, selves will be whole, our fathers and mothers will have given us enough.

I tried to tell Bliss that, but she wasn't buying it. No way did we get enough, no possible way. We were just getting started. Losing your father is hard at any age. Had I lost my father at a very young age, I do think that he would have given me enough of a compass for my own development, but then I would have missed so much of his life. I'm so lucky to get to grow up and old with my father, to witness each of us change and mature. But Tommy's response to the loss of his father somehow has to be the path. For now, I can't say that I got enough, or that we got enough. I can't pretend that there's any possible reason to cut a man's life so short.

I am perhaps most sad not when I'm missing him for me or for us, but when I'm missing him for him. "We miss him, but he's missing his whole life," I told my yoga teacher, Jordan. A Buddhist, he disagreed. "No, in fact, he lived his whole life, as it turns out. And he lived it very well." Help us have enough.

JUNE 19, 2017
Stepfathers Are the Best

"Stepfathers are the best," my neighbor Karyn says, aching with the loss of Tommy. She is moving back to her hometown, following her husband to a new job. She's sad to leave this pocket of neighborly utopia that operates as a real village. I'll miss her too, not just for her easy way and Friday night bonfires, but also for the sound of her three boys, endlessly rolling around in the yard like puppies. She'd worry about the noise, early on weekend mornings, and about the never-ending football game in our shared back-yard, but Tommy and I assured her we loved it. "No," I finally said, "You don't understand; the sound of boys playing is literally music to Tommy's ears." And it was. Tommy's three boys, now young men, were the sun of his solar system. He had been a father for twenty-three years when he met us, the most important part of his identity. The sound of boys in the yard reminded him of his happiest hours, building a hockey rink every winter behind their house, the boys and their friends spending countless hours skating before and after school.

Last weekend Karyn had been house hunting, and her stepfather had driven her around three towns so she could get the lay of the land, patiently waiting in the car while she went to open house after open house. Who are these men who marry our mothers and enter our lives? Until I met Tommy, I don't remember anyone really talking about stepfathers. But once I did, the stories came out. Adult women spoke with tenderness, respect, and gratitude toward these men who had become beloved parts of their lives. Few of them called these men stepfathers—father or dad would do just fine. One of Tommy's greatest points of pride was the way Bliss would say, "Bye, Daddy; hi, Tommy!" or "Bye, Tommy; hi, Daddy!" without hesitation.

Liv, Bliss, and I went wedding-dress shopping in February. Sophie was back at school, so we FaceTimed with her from the dressing room. I had seen a dress I was interested in, and tried it on first. Perfect. We went through many others, coming back to the original choice. It was *the* dress, and the decision was simple and clear. We met Tommy for dinner on the way home, a midweek celebration. We talked about the wedding, our family, what they would call him. They called him Tommy, but they said they already thought of him as a father.

I can't speak about what Tommy may have meant to my girls, because my heart breaks more than I can bear. I ache for them. But I can say, for now, how gracefully and wholly he became essential to our lives. If you ever ran into him, you couldn't help but hear about each child and her pursuits in great detail. His love for me was undeniable, but I was only part of the package. This pain is too raw to describe, so I will stick to the stories told by others, in the secret confidence of those who experience great love and family life in nontraditional ways.

JUNE 22, 2017
Humble Warrior

Today is a "humble warrior" day. I imagine this yoga pose is not popular, but I was glad to do it this morning. You stand in warrior one and then bow to the ground. Most people in class cannot touch their head to the ground, so there is a sort of uncomfortable limbo. A combination of loose joints and a nearly daily practice means that I can touch my forehead easily to the ground, and when I do, I can feel the stress from my body, especially from my brain and eyes, pour into the floor. "Strength and surrender," Tara says in this pose. Strength and surrender, humble warrior.

Tommy's humility was a big part of who he was. When we were writing his obituary, I found a box of keepsakes and started pulling out the stacks of awards. His son marveled, "He was not just the best at one thing, he was the best at everything." The only award I had heard of was the Ernie Davis Award, named for the 1961 Heisman Trophy winner from Elmira, New York. It goes to the top high school football player from Chemung County, for character on and off the field.

More important, Ernie Davis was Tommy Niles's idol. Ernie Davis's father died when he was a baby, and he moved around before settling in Elmira at age twelve with his mother and stepfather. He played baseball, basketball, and football at Elmira Free Academy and was named All-American. Several colleges recruited him to play football, and he chose Syracuse to follow in the footsteps of his childhood idol, Jim Brown. He became the first African American winner of the Heisman Trophy in 1961. But as he started his NFL career with the Cleveland Browns, he was diagnosed with leukemia and died a year later at age twenty-three.

Tommy told this story again and again, adding new pieces with every telling: How badly Ernie wanted to play one game with teammate Jim Brown. How badly the world wanted that too. How the coaches wouldn't let him, because he was simply not healthy enough. About him meeting John F. Kennedy. About how he faced his illness, returning to Elmira for treatment. About the racism he faced as a black man at Syracuse and in the NFL. About his humanity and humility. About his grace and strength of character.

I went with Tommy to visit the since-named Ernie Davis Academy in Elmira and saw the legendary football field of Tommy's youth and the sculpture of Ernie Davis at the entry. I understood what this man meant to Tommy, and I imagined the pride he must have felt at receiving the Ernie Davis Award as a high school senior.

But there was more to that story. There was another athlete in Tommy's class, perhaps an even better one. In the spring of their senior year, this friend, who was African American, got into some kind of trouble. He didn't win the Ernie Davis Award and didn't go to college; instead he went to prison. End of story. Except, Tommy said, his story was far from over. He got a good job, married his high school sweetheart, and had children and grandchildren. He was, and is, an honorable man.

I have no doubt that Tommy deserved the award. But that is not really the point. Tommy had an inner strength and confidence and was comfortable in his skin. But he also had a clear-eye view of reality, including life's subtle and not-so-subtle complexities that confer advantages and disadvantages.

I am not sure where humility comes from. I think Tommy's humility came from having a deep curiosity about and respect for other people. His heroes were always the stars of his stories, whether they were great historical figures or his own children.

I bow my head to you, my humble warrior, and am deeply grateful that when I do, the floor is there to hold me.

JUNE 25, 2017
Wounded Warrior

When the EMTs arrived, they were fairly casual, making jokes and asking questions. Did they know immediately that Tommy was having a heart attack? It's hard to tell; I certainly didn't know. Have you felt like this before, they asked? Yes, two and a half years ago, he said.

Tommy was referring to the day of our first date. When he first told me this story, I thought it was cute—like he had pregame jitters. After all, he had been building me up in his mind for more than a year. He used to tell me that before football games, he wouldn't eat for two days, and that he would always throw up before the game. It wasn't until later that I understood he was really quite sick that day—it may have been an anxiety attack, which can feel similar to a heart attack, I don't know.

After I wrote this week about my humble warrior, I started to think about my wounded warrior, the Tommy I met in 2015. I don't use those words lightly. Tommy supported the Wounded Warrior Project. He was spared combat time during his service, and he had the utmost respect and compassion for those who weren't. But it's fair to say that Tommy was a shadow of himself when we met. Separated from his family, living in a generic apartment complex, this man who identified as a husband, father, homeowner, coach, dog-lover, and pillar of the community was lost. He had given up the houses in Needham and Nantucket—no dogs allowed in the apartment; no tools needed there either. Some may have believed a false rumor that he had cheated and abandoned his family. For the first time in his life, he stood separate from the parents at hockey games. The man whose team had won the Little League championships eight years running felt cast out of the heart of the community. He had his old friends, his music, his thoughts.

He wasn't terribly healthy, either. He barely slept. He was up at 3 or 4 a.m. every day. His doctor wanted him to lose 25 pounds. He had a broken heart, a broken tooth, and a fragility that belied his strong and handsome frame. It took me awhile to understand this. How could I know that this gorgeous, smiling, lovely man was hurting so much? He was coping as well as he could, of course. He had two hotels under construction in Boston and had kept the projects on schedule despite those 100-plus inches of snow. He did anything he could for his kids. He was funny, lively, kind, and, again, so gorgeous. His face made you feel good, his friend Doug said—his smile alone was a gift. "Tommy was the closest thing to Jesus Christ I have ever known," he said, "but he just felt things more than the rest of us." The disappointments, the jabs, the losses.

In May of our first year together, we celebrated his birthday. The boys came for dinner—their first time to the house. Tommy manned the grill, ever the host. Bliss asked him about his favorite candy—Whoppers, hard to make into a cake. Instead she made elaborate chocolate cupcakes with Reese's candy. A few days later we took a weekend birthday trip to New Orleans. This was our first big trip together, and it was transformational. We stayed at one of my friends' beautiful houses in the Garden District. We rented bikes and rode all over town. We ate, drank, made love.

One night, after a great evening and dinner out, we went to bed and set the alarm for midnight to go down to the jazz clubs on Frenchman Street. We had an absolute blast. I remember Tommy accidentally bumping into a big guy at the bar, who took offense. Within minutes, though, they were best buds. The man had recently gotten engaged and was talking to his fiancé on the phone, assuring her that he was not drunk (he was). Tommy told the guy that he would be the luckiest man on earth to be engaged to me. Close to 2 a.m., the sky opened in a flash flood and water filled the street. Tommy threw me on his back and ran. I had a white T-shirt on and felt like a girl. He kept that photo of us, soaked and smiling, on his dresser.

That weekend, the layers also started to peel back. He shared how deeply lost and heartbroken he had felt. His boys were always his focus, his happy place. Dogs helped; the beach helped. After his separation, he found some comfort in a small group at church. He listened to music. Tommy was a magnet for women, but his brother admonished him, "What do you need women for? Just play guitar." He played.

We got up late the day after the rainstorm and were walking to a café when he stopped and put a hand in his pocket. "I want to give you something." "Oh no!" I panicked, thinking it was a ring. I wanted it to be a ring. I didn't want it to be a ring. We had known each other only two months! I knew he was "the one," but I was scared; it was too fast—don't ruin it! It wasn't a ring. It was a heart-shaped stone he had found on the beach a few years earlier. He recited a poem that conveyed his heartbreak. How I wish I could remember the words of that poem.

I watched him become calmer, fitter, and more relaxed. He started to sleep again. We would still wake up at 5:10 a.m. on weekdays but were usually in bed by 10 p.m. We slept late on the weekends, read the *New York Times*, and stayed in bed until noon on Sundays. He cut out gluten (except for the occasional beer or birthday cake) and said his mind felt better than ever. He finished the Sunday crossword puzzle, usually by Tuesday. He lost 20 pounds and worked out four or five times a week. He gave up his car commute and took the train, walked, and rented city bikes. I gave him a bright blue helmet for Christmas. A few weeks before he died, he played his first round of golf of the year. He and Doug "kept the tee" for eighteen straight holes, surprising their competition who played every day.

Tommy moved into our house and had a real home again. By the time we finished Bohemia, I can honestly say he felt like he lived in heaven on earth. The night he died, the boys were to come to dinner. The girls loved him and were game for anything. They listened to his stories, toured his projects, went to his building openings, celebrated his successes, cooked with him, and traveled with him. He took us to a Patriots game, and we carved out time on our schedules to watch every single game together, simply because watching football with him was pure pleasure. Liv knew all the stats and discussed every trade and score. He was the proudest parent at the high school hockey banquet when Liv won an all-star award. Sophie went off to college, but we all visited her for a long weekend in Denver. The weekend before he died, he watched and recorded her lacrosse games in Salt Lake City, sharing stories of her accomplishments with his friends. He called Bliss his "warrior of love," and her ability to love so expansively calmed and energized him. He was her "Tommy NILES!" and came home to her greeting and hug every day. Love. Love is what heals.

What if he had had a heart attack on March 11, 2015, the day we met, instead of that day in May two years later? What if he had missed this last phase of his life? "We got everything but time." But was it enough? Could he have been healthier, more loved, more fit? My mother says he died as happy as a man could be. My yoga teacher says we should all be so lucky. I know in my heart that our wounded warrior was whole, his battle scars only making him stronger. I wish to God that he had been able to live into that wholeness over time, to enjoy and relish this time of his life. I wish to God that he had us longer, that we had him longer.

2

Our Word Shall Still Be Joy,

Shall Still Be Joy

JUNE 26, 2017
The In-Between

There is a scene in one of my favorite books, *Hopscotch*, in which the main character, Traveler, says to Talita, "We almost dreamed the same dreams." Tormented lover, he could not reconcile that when they fell asleep, heads touching, the intimacy of their love would dissolve into separate dreaming lives. On wakening, they would share their dreams, and he felt jealous of this part of her that was inaccessible to him. One night, Traveler thought, they almost dreamed the same dream—the details were different, but the essence was the same. But Talita didn't get it; she laughed at him.

For a brief time in yoga, Tommy would do half pigeon with his left leg bent, right leg extended, when the teacher called for the right leg bent, left leg extended, which is what I did. He would put the sole of his left foot on the sole of my right foot, and they pressed together, giving us each some resistance and an extra hip stretch. I thought we must have formed a sort of heart shape on the ground with our bodies. Eventually it stopped, and we never spoke about it. I wonder sometimes whether that had been intentional. Did he know he was making a heart shape of our bodies or was it just my imagination?

Sarah tells me that over time, I will need to integrate this loss, love, and grief into myself. That made sense, and I thought that if this loss was going to be a part of me forever, I had better make sure that it was more love than loss, more love than bitterness, more love than sorrow.

What does integration mean when the love and grief already feel like a part of me, without clear boundaries? "I see you as intertwined vines, like the image of your legs wrapped around one another in bed. Could that be a metaphor, too, for your spirits?" Jeannie, my friend and Reiki practitioner, asks when I describe this vertiginous feeling of falling in love, now more than ever, of not being able to separate his soul from mine, of his spirit leaving his body as I held it in my hands.

For now, I cannot tell where the edges are.

JUNE 28, 2017
The Earth and Its People Should Celebrate Today

Happy Birthday—such simple words. My birthday today. Thank goodness for Facebook, which has reinvigorated the idea of birthdays; you can get hundreds of well wishes. But who remembers the birthday card? I had never been a card writer, shame on me. In fact, I am seriously perplexed about how on earth I was able to manufacture this sweet card on Tommy's birthday, the first that we spent together.

> May 25, 2015. I wrote:
>
> Dear Tommy,
>
> Happy Birthday! And thank you for sharing it with me. I couldn't be happier than to spend a few precious days with you. You are optimism, you are open heart, you are generosity, and it is such a blessing to me.
>
> I love this yoga card because this is my pose—the pose that I envision myself at the fullest expression of me. When I am doing it and when I'm just thinking about it. Strong roots, centered middle and endless stretch to the heavens. What I think about you, and about us.
>
> Happy birthday and many many happy ones to come.
>
> Much love,
>
> xo Katie

A drawing of tree pose is on the cover, *the pose that I envision myself at the fullest expression of me.* What was it about Tommy that brought out the fullest expression of me? I have since gotten dozens (dare I say hundreds?) of letters from people who say he brought out the fullest expression of them. A colleague wrote, "Tom had the unique ability to make you feel special no matter what you were saying. He gave you his full attention and he was always present with you."

> June 28, 2015
>
> Happy Birthday Katie Swenson!
>
> I feel so happy and blessed to be able to be with you and share this special day

with you, with all of your loved ones at this very amazing place on earth.

The earth and its people should celebrate today just for the love, energy, care and irrepressible passions you have given to make it a better place.

You are one in a billion Katie . . .

Thank you for opening up your life to me. I look forward so much to many, many beautiful happy birthdays to come . . .

". . . And I thank you to my God

Now I've finally got it right

And I'll fight with all my heart

with all my soul

with all my might. . . ."

Matisyahu

All my love,

xo Tommy

JUNE 30, 2017
Time Expands for Us

"Time expands for us," Tommy would say. In the early days of our relationship, time seemed to shift its shape, slow down, make room for us. "There always seems to be enough time for us," he would say, amazed that we could make love and catch the train, make love and catch the plane, make love and make the eggs, get to class, get to work.

Except that while time expands for us, it is also falling in on me. A friend, a widow of nine years whose young husband collapsed at a friend's wedding, with a three-month-old baby at home, is now remarried to a man she loves and with whom she has two more children. She says the shock of pain still comes, unbidden, nine years later, sometimes finding her in bed next to her beloved second husband.

Time heals, they say. Perhaps that healing time is the moment between love and ecstasy, or between pain and suffering. The shock of pain strikes when it wants. That's why grievers say that recovery is not day by day but minute by minute. Minutes count, seconds count. In that second that pain hits, I wonder, can I make time expand, just at that moment? Can I change the effect of that pain? Sometimes the pain leads to tears; they can be pure tears or cloudy tears; they can be sobs or silent; they can rage or be a dull ache. All that pain can lead to suffering, but I don't want that. I will take the pain, but I don't want to suffer, to let the pain spill over into despair and bitterness. I want to expand that moment, make a choice, take a breath, see a new way.

At yoga, Tommy is always in my mind's eye. The shape of his shoulders and the way the blue shirt would fall across his back. I can still see the ripples in the fabric, the way the hem hung against his black shorts. The image of his profile next to me or across the room always flooded me with endorphins. Now as I see that image in my mind, I am overcome with sadness. Does it have to be that way? If that image once gave me a humming joy, can I retrieve that feeling, even in the face of loss? Can I make the time and space expand around it, to soothe myself with the feeling of joy in that image, and not feel the sorrow?

I don't know, but I feel like I have been training my whole life for this split second—when pain hits, to take the pause, take the breath, steady the heart, and still the mind. To feel the pain, feel the love in that pain, but maybe let the suffering go.

JULY 3, 2017
A Hundred Positive Things

At my cousin Christian's funeral a few years ago, I gave his brother, Jonathan, a long hug and said, "Could I be your sister, and you my little brother?" Christian's outrageously early death—at not quite forty-four years of age, with a wife and two young sons—was awful in every way. Christian and Jonathan are my only cousins; Christian was a few years younger than I, and Jonathan a few years younger than him. Christian was a true Renaissance man. He studied art history and worked as a curator before going to business school and doing well on Wall Street. When I crossed paths with him in our early twenties in downtown New York, he was in between art and finance, his natural talent and ardent curiosity leading to an intensely rich life. He was a modern-day Thomas Jefferson, growing heirloom vegetables and planting an orchard upstate, cooking like a professional chef, and learning piano with his young son while managing a demanding international career.

Jonathan and I hadn't seen each other often as adults, but Christian was his only sibling and he readily accepted my offer. Now he calls me Big Sis, which I take as a compliment. We started to get to know each other. A hesitant texter at first, he now texts me about everything from sports to family news.

What we didn't know at that moment at Christian's funeral was that we would both experience this horrible early grieving. Jonathan had heard all about Tommy, of course, and got to know him at our grandmother's ninety-ninth birthday last fall. We met again this year for Easter at our grandmother's house in Washington, DC, and spent a fantastic day with family, Tommy playing catch with Jonathan's sons, Finn, nine, and Whit, five. Tommy was in his element, patiently letting the game forge a bond between them. Jonathan and Heather were the first out-of-town guests to buy plane tickets to our wedding, securing tickets to Fenway for the Thursday afternoon Sox game.

It's heartbreaking for me to think about Jonathan telling his boys that Tommy had died—far too much loss for them at such a young age. But Jonathan's comment about grieving his brother resonated more than I could have imagined: "There will be a hundred positive things that occur as a result of Tommy's death." Nobody says that.

According to Jonathan, Christian was a great guitar player. After Christian died, Jonathan pushed himself to practice the guitar. The songs he wrote helped him express his feelings about his brother's life and death. He even recorded an album. Never in his life would he have imagined recording an album, but how better to get close to his brother, to make something out of his death?

What I am sure everybody knows, but I am just learning, is that death is so final. These beloved brothers, husbands, and fathers don't come back after they have died. It's unimaginable, really. So, if death is final, Jonathan asks, does it get to have the last word? Not on his watch. With two pairs of next-generation brothers growing up, you bet he's going to talk about his brother, tell the stories, laugh at the funny moments, tell the jokes. Ever the younger brother, he may even throw his older brother under the bus. And he is going to make something positive out of this loss. His brother may or may not have been the better guitar player, but Jonathan is sure as hell going to make the album. Remember, tell, create, spin yarns, write lyrics, make something living and lasting that defies death. That way death is not allowed to be only an end, but also a beginning. Can a hundred good things happen as a result of Tommy's death? I hadn't thought before to count the good things, but I just might start making a list. From what I have seen so far, it's not impossible to imagine.

JULY 4, 2017
The Seamlessness of Him

While lying in shavasana, Tommy would transport himself to the swim dock at Taconnet. What better feeling is there than the heaviness of a relaxed body, combined with the weightlessness of rocking with the tide on the raft, warm sun on wet skin. I have been coming to this island in Belgrade Lakes, Maine, for thirty-five years, long before I knew Tommy. And yet now, he is in every view, every cold shock of clear water, and every activity. He is fishing with Bliss, playing tennis with me. It is his mountain to hike, his canoe race to win (good luck, maybe next year?), his cooler that is missing.

Tommy became family so seamlessly that it's hard to remember a time before him. What is that magical ability he had to fit right in? I know our relationship started with us, and that "we" were at the center of it always. But like so many things now, I can no longer see the edges of anything, where he started and I left off, or where we started and our worlds began.

I think of his years of practice integrating with families, his ability to be the favorite guest, the first invited back, the one with a special seat next to the head of the table. I swear that if you asked who among his college friends had invited Tommy over for Thanksgiving dinner, at least a half-dozen hands would go up. The bigger the family, the better, it seemed. Maybe he was at the Robustellis with Chris's nine brothers and sisters and their gregarious parents and extended family, Mr. Robustelli taking Tommy Niles to task on the basketball court. But maybe he was with the Coluccis and their five kids, or the Haggertys and their nine.

My mom is still wondering when he'll finish the trim on her skylights, and she can't stop thinking of projects for him to do, forgetting, in that moment, that he is not there. Oh, yeah, he pulled that "bring my tools" trick on her too. The first time we came to these sweet little cabins in Maine, he brought fishing rods, beer, and good will. But then he realized this place was a weekend warrior's dream. On subsequent visits he packed his truck with tools and would spend mornings puttering, fixing, planning. Heaven.

Up here in Maine, where he is in every sunrise and sunset, every ripple on the lake, I can't help but wonder at how fully he penetrated the lives of my family.

JULY 5, 2017
Elmira

We visited Elmira, New York, last summer, the legendary setting of Tommy Niles's youth. A big sign at the city entrance reads, "Honoring the Past, Building the Future," with oversized figures of local stars Brian Williams, Hal Roach, Mark Twain, Eileen Collins, John Jones, Tommy Hilfiger, and of course Tommy's idol, Ernie Davis. Elmira hit its peak around 1950 with about 50,000 residents and a large number of corporate headquarters and plants. It was still thriving in 1960, the year Tommy was born, with just over 46,000 residents, but the next decade saw a 15 percent population decrease, and then another 11 percent decrease the decade after that. Major corporations left town in the 1970s when Hurricane Agnes hit in 1972, wiping out whole sections of the city, which were later abandoned or subject to the devastation of urban renewal.

Tommy's dad was busy that year. An electrician with the city public-works department, he was on the front lines of the rescue and repair teams. He invited displaced strangers to stay at the modest house at 1010 Hoffman. Their home was always a central figure in Tommy's stories. When we went to see it that summer, it was not particularly well cared for. The hospital had expanded around it, buying up properties for parking lots and not investing in the neighborhood character. But the house felt familiar from his stories—a simple, three-bedroom Victorian with a great yard and a hoop in the driveway. I'd heard tales of the neighborhood kids, trouble coming and going, fighting, playing. The garage his dad built.

After his dad died, his mom had to sell the house. Robbie Brewer and his dad came to look, and Robbie and Tommy played basketball outside while the sale was underway. Leave it to Tommy to form a lifelong friendship in a moment like that. The Nileses left the piano for the Brewers, but Tommy and his siblings were welcome to come play, and Tommy spent lots of time there throughout high school. Robbie and his wife, Karen, visited us last summer, bearing extravagant engagement gifts.

Tommy met Andrew Colucci when they were twelve, the summer after his father's death. They were two of fewer than a dozen kids in the gifted program at the middle school and were in the same classes for grades seven through nine. Throughout the tough middle school and high school years, they found a haven in each other's homes. Tommy was the baby of his family and had doting, musical sisters, although they had left home by the time he reached high school. Andrew loved going to Tommy's new house and loved his mom too. The house was a craftsman bungalow just a few blocks away and always smelled like homemade cookies. Andrew's large Italian household had a different vibe. It was an architect-designed, modern house outside town near the monastery, and a haven for philosophical conversations, authentic Italian cooking, modern art, free expression, and social activism. Tommy made himself at home and beloved there.

Andrew's mom was a progressive liberal, marching for civil rights and against the Vietnam War. Mrs. Colucci had gone to Catholic University, gotten married, and had six children, and when the boys met, she was pursuing her master's degree at the School for Human Ecology at Cornell.

Andrew remembers telling his mom that Tommy's father had died the previous summer. Riding in the back seat, Andrew listened as his mom asked Tommy about his father. Tommy was matter-of-fact about his death, and Andrew could hear the concern in his mother's voice. She had lost her father too, but to prison—he ran an underground gambling ring. Tommy, marked as special, became a regular at the Colucci house.

Mrs. Colucci took the thirteen-year-old boys with her to Cornell so they could experience the beautiful campus where they might attend college one day. She asked them questions that made them think, urging them to stake out a position and explain why. She had considered law school but chose human ecology because she could reach more people, she thought; what did Tommy think? Andrew marveled at Tommy's ability to converse confidently with his mom.

During those rides, Mrs. Colucci often talked about what she was learning, but she also asked the boys about their day on campus. What was it that you liked best in the Johnson Art Museum (the answer was the giant knight)? Do you like the modern architecture? How did it make you feel? She didn't let the boys get away with "it was cool"; they had to be specific. Andrew recalled that Tommy was always on point and effortless, adding some extra detail or connection that was outside the box or fall-off-your-chair funny. Tommy did most of the talking, and Andrew loved listening from the back seat.

On one trip, Tommy bought a George Carlin album and proceeded to memorize every skit. He was a natural mimic, down to the voice accents. This was new for Andrew, who had never laughed so hard in his life. Tommy moved on to Monty Python, and thus began a comedy routine that lasted forty-five years. It was an outlet for expressing himself through various performance arts, from music to speaking, drawing, and cartoons. "He shared so selflessly with me; he knew how it delighted and filled me up," Andrew says.

For years, Tommy would leave songs on Andrew's voicemail. Andrew could tell how he was doing through the tone and rhythm. He felt the joy and heard the pain. For forty-five glorious years, from their first ride to Cornell until just recently, Tommy performed for Andrew.

The last song Tommy left as a message was "Take Me to Church," Andrew says, still getting the shivers. It came from a place he had not heard before, textured, rich, and thick. There was a major shift, something powerful occurring. "My lover's got humor / She's the giggle at a funeral / Knows everybody's disapproval / I should've worshiped her sooner . . ."

I love hearing these stories about the development of this boy, raised by the proverbial village, who had such natural gifts. Chief among them was the gift of engaging and validating others. He made you feel good about being you.

JULY 14, 2017
Sanity

It's hard to be forever the fiancé, rather than the wife that Tommy wanted me to be. I know the truth of us, as do his friends and family, but the fact remains that we were not yet married. I had no legal status.

Bates and Coman had no legal status when Coman died, either—that would have been impossible. But twenty-five years of friendship were embedded in their family and social structures in a way that honored their relationship, even if it was not named. Bates wrote a letter after Coman's death in 1915, "For Katharine Coman's Family and Innermost Circle of Friends." She begins, "Because it fell to me, in the friendship which remains my joy and blessing, to know the successive stages of Katharine's long suffering, I would like to set down in simplest fashion and only for the eyes of those who have love's right to see, the history of her illness."

The intimacy of this letter binds me to these women and their love, and to this death experienced in the very room I inhabit. She continues, "As I lifted the shade that she might enjoy the flush in the sky, I did not yet realize that this pale-rose dawn was the last those dear grey eyes would ever see." And I see the pink dawn of Tommy's last morning, his eyes meeting mine as he expressed his love for me.

Some days I lose track of what I know to be real. I use the word "fiancé" to legitimize our relationship and the extent of my grief, but in fact the legal status is immaterial. In worrying about what others think, I start to question what I know to be true. Loss of the most beloved on earth still pales in comparison to the loss of your own sanity.

The chaos of grief, of my own and others, swirling, makes me question everything. Others claim different truths—their own version of him, their own idea of who he was and what ought to have happened after he died. I wanted to have an autopsy done. I want to have a marker for his ashes. I was not yet next of kin; I am not included in these decisions. But I know what I know to be true is actually true.

I want to believe I know what Tommy would have wanted. I know his likely first response, his second response; I know what he would say the next day. And now that I know what I know, I will not allow myself to question that knowledge any longer; I cannot. I understand that my faith in that knowledge will be tested, likely again and again. I also know that I can come back to this truth.

I wish he were here to voice his opinion, make the plan, choose his gravesite. Would it be the Niles family cemetery in Pennsylvania, the one he visited with his family? He also sent photos of a Niles gravesite near the University of Rhode Island, his alma mater. And pictures of a Niles headstone at Arlington Cemetery we visited last Easter. I imagine a headstone at the historic cemetery on Nantucket, his favorite landscape on earth. I am not a part of these decisions.

I wish we could discuss it together, as we did with anything important. I wish we could unpack it together, go over the argument, the evidence, the details. I wish we could consider the question from multiple perspectives. But just because we can't do that, now, in this moment, doesn't erase the countless times we did that. It doesn't negate what we learned together and what I know to be true.

Questioning is itself a crisis. But it's not necessarily a crisis that needs to continue. I do know what he would have wanted, in my deepest place. Even if I am tempted by some alternative view, I will not stop knowing.

JULY 19, 2017
Vows

The forecast is out for July 22—85 degrees and sunny, a perfect day for a wedding, just as we had hoped. We had spoken of this day for so long that our marriage plans are somehow fully merged into most of my memories of Tommy. The first summer we met, we made the eleven-hour drive to Canada to visit Andrew Colucci and his wife, Jeanette, and friends at Jeanette's family's lake house. About forty-five minutes from home, Tommy asked me if I had my passport. Whoops! We went home to get it and started our journey again. I remember the amazement he felt that we could just do that, just turn around, start again, not really caring about the time lost, since it provided more time for us to be together in the car.

After the border crossing, somewhere in Ontario, we began talking about marriage, family, weddings. We talked about our own weddings, others' weddings, a wedding on Nantucket. We were so deep in conversation that we missed the turn! Eleven hours into our drive, we were so enmeshed in each other and in our future that we had to retrace the last thirty minutes of the drive.

Tommy wanted it all. A traditional wedding with out-of-town guests, a fancy dress, and dancing. We planned a taco truck instead of sit-down dinner, a DJ instead of a band. We considered different possibilities, like having a legal ceremony separate from a party. But in the end, the only thing he cared about was that we be married and exchange vows. He said he wrote our marriage vows in his mind nonstop. What, oh what, was he writing? What would I give to have worked through that process with him, to have written those vows to and for each other?

July 22 will now be a "Celebration of Love and Family," and I know that is what Tommy would have wanted under these circumstances. I can see that the easiest thing to do would be to crawl under the covers with a heavy dose of sedatives. But instead, I will commit myself to my vows, on this day and every day going forward, knowing that I will succeed and fail at them, as all people do, but also knowing that they will guide me and give me courage.

JULY 20, 2017

Resilience, the Word of the Day

My office is busy. I'm not there—my work has given me the ultimate gift of time, but I'm getting scattered updates. My Boston-based team is amazing, everyone stepping up in ways big and small. A crew was in town for the official launch of our new climate and cultural resilience program. It was so great to see everyone, some new recruits and collaborators from other cities. I went to the office briefly, but then they came to me, gathering at the Scarab, the best gift they could give me.

The big news today was that we received hundreds of applications for the Collaborative Action grants. These are small grants, started a few years ago with help from a foundation whose mission is to promote love, forgiveness, and compassion in the world through design. Yup. We read, talked, and learned about love, forgiveness, and compassion—what are these things, and how do they operate at a personal and community level? How does a community build resilience in the face of injustice, loss, destructive climate events? What are the effects of poverty on human development, and how can love, compassion, and forgiveness promote healing?

I am living my own version of a Collaborative Action grant, or what we call "love grants." The trauma of Tommy's death is raw and grueling to me and to his family and close friends, but it is also a community loss, as it always is. And our community, local and all over the country, is rallying to help heal. The neighborhood is in full swing. Beth organizes dozens of moms so that lunches for the girls arrive daily. Molly comes to watch Bliss's game. Dave changes the gas tank for the grill. Meagan brings the baby. Lisa rubs my back. Johnny starts plotting how to organize the workbench. Stephanie comes to make the bed. And, from afar, Sherry-Lea sends the softest shawl with pockets like a comfy sweater. Books, lots of them—*Healing after Loss*, *A Thousand Mornings*, *Option B*, *Say Her Name*, *The Year of Magical Thinking*—waiting for the winter ahead. Cards, so many cards, words, stories, love. It matters. How do you create the context for healing? Nothing can change the essential devastating fact. He apparently, unbelievably, is not coming home.

Lynn organized the hockey moms to come last night, each bearing food and drink, each with a small hole in her heart for Tommy's particular brand of kindness, his way of listening, asking specifically after you or your family, remembering the details from the last conversation. His unabashed love, hopes, and dreams for the boys, sharing stories from their lives. His attentiveness and pride in the girls' daily accomplishments or antics.

Everyone wanted to relive the last time they saw him; for many it was that weekend before he died, when I was in Salt Lake with Sophie, blessed time for us two, made possible by Tommy being at home. Many of his text messages to me over those few days were sweet nothings: "Hi babe . . . wow, what a warrior athlete . . . Girls all well, bliss in bed, liv working late and 6 am practice plus junior boat cruise . . . Bliss and team rocked it in lacrosse . . . g'night baby . . . xxo . . . Good morning sunshine . . . ," and so on. Now I get to hear more of the story.

One mom tells me that on Friday night, Tommy volunteered to take the eighth graders to lacrosse practice, standing in the rain to watch them play. There was a great hill next to the field, and Tommy let the girls go sledding on the slick grass afterward. He took them for ice cream on the way home, listening to the Celtics game in the car with his posse of girls.

There was a Tommy sighting at Fells Market, the local shop, a casual and sweet conversation, a thoughtful inquiry. He walked the neighborhood, stopping to chat, made a plan to listen to records in the barn with Johnny. Amy and Guido had been building a beautiful stone wall for weeks. Hundreds of people have stopped to admire, inquire about their methods. Tommy went by on Saturday, but what was remarkable about that visit? Of those hundreds of casual visitors, they say, he was the only person who asked if he could help.

What lesson is kindness? When you lose a man like that, he stays with you forever, says one of the hockey moms. Tommy's essential characteristic was kindness. And now, we are surrounded by the reverberation of kindness from every aspect of our lives, washing over us, holding us. It doesn't change the pain, but it does make it easier to bear. It doesn't change the depth of grief, but it makes grieving possible. These enormous kindnesses give me the space to love and grieve.

Writing is my happiest time now, and I have been given the gift of time and space for that, a reprieve from work to just be. It has turned out to be the very best way for me to think of him, respect him, learn about him, and love him without the overwhelming sorrow that accompanies me day and night. People read and respond with kindness. Love, forgiveness, and compassion are alive in the world.

JULY 21, 2017

The Coffee Dance

Mornings are when I miss him the most. I know in part it's just the most natural blurriness on waking, the half-conscious state of where am I? What day is it? Did that really happen? We've experienced that our whole lives in so many different forms, so it's natural, but now the consequences of waking are grueling. Ugh. Is he really still gone? Is this really my reality? Do I have to face this again?

But it's more than that. Evenings were family or social time. Daytime was work or activities. But morning was our sacred space, and we stretched out that time, enlarged it. Every day that I woke up with him felt like a gift in that moment.

When we first met, he barely slept. I was used to waking up early, my alarm set for 5:10 a.m. on weekdays. But he'd start stirring around 4 a.m. He had gotten used to very few hours of sleep, going to bed late and waking early—insomnia, worry, beating the traffic, hitting the jobsite, getting there with the crew. He started going to bed earlier, sleeping later, enjoying being in bed with me.

He told Doug that when he heard me take out my night guard, he took that sound as an invitation, which it was. Least sexy item on the planet, that anti-teeth-grinding device, somehow transformed into a marker of domestic intimacy. We didn't make love only in the morning, and we didn't make love every morning, but most days I'd reach my foot out as I sensed him stirring, and we would begin the day together.

He told me when we first met that he would bring me coffee in bed every day for the rest of my life. He kept that promise, I guess. When we designed Bohemia, we made a "coffee kitchen," putting together a stainless-steel IKEA camp sink, mini-fridge, and floating shelf. The simplest and most luxurious gift ever, the ultimate indulgence. Tommy took pleasure and pride in the production. One cup at a time, pour-over style. Electric tea kettle, Peet's coffee, cone filter, large white cup, half-and-half for me, black for him. He made my cup first, delighting in the foamy richness of that first blush of ground coffee and hot water, the sludgy bloom and smell that rose and made me sit up in bed in eager anticipation.

But perhaps the part I miss more than I can comprehend is watching his body move through our space, watching his coffee dance, ritual choreography. Turn to the left to sit up, feet touching floor. Reach for glasses and adjust. Hand through hair, putting down the cowlick (the hair—a whole topic of its own!). First steps, slightly heavy, picking up grace with a few strides, moving fluidly after about a dozen steps, rounding the bend, pulling at the waistband of his shorts. That beautiful body gliding in my imagination. When I was lying down, his chest was my favorite moment of him—shoulder, chest, my hand, my head—the most perfect resting place on earth. But when he moved, I got it all—back, shoulders, arms moving, legs, feet testing the ground.

It's still curious to me that the last morning, a morning normal in its absolute perfection, he talked to me about my body moving through space. I stayed in bed, captive audience to the coffee dance. From my spot, I can see the whole room in Bohemia: the eastern light filtering in behind me, the western sky picking up the colors of the day. When the trees are not in bloom, I can see the horizon through the 20-foot stretch of window, and that day, the combination of new buds and partial leaves delivered a tapestry of pinks.

He came toward me, moving carefully, cup hot and nearly full to the brim, guarding against spilling. Hand back to hair, glasses adjust, cup of love in hand. Make room on the side table, move last night's water glass, last night's wine glass, the book maybe, the glasses, the night guard, make a space to set coaster and cup.

Normally on this day, a Wednesday, he'd be off to Providence early to meet Joe and Fernando for breakfast, a 7 a.m. start time. Normally, he'd set my coffee down and go around the corner to dress. But that day, he skipped breakfast with his friends; he would stay with me and we would go to yoga together. He came back to bed.

On that day he talked about the choreography of me, his world tipping back onto its axis as he watched me move. I had only moved from lying down to sitting up. He'd say that when I was under the covers, asleep, sometimes he'd have a moment of panic. With my body stretched out, he couldn't always tell if I was there. I remember the physical surge of love I felt as he was talking to me. Delivering my coffee, telling me about his love for me, my body, my movement. I remember the out-of-body experience of thinking that he was saying what I was thinking about him, rather than what he was thinking about me, roles reversed, or merged as we merged, again.

JULY 23, 2017
Wedding Day

The to-have-been wedding day at last arrived. We had planned to hold the wedding at my parents' house on Sabrina Lake, with a big dance tent down near the water. But this gathering would be at our house. Tommy loved how parties just seemed to happen there. It was a house designed for people, gatherings of all shapes and sizes. The house has an extra-wide center hall. Alice Friedman recounts that when Katharine Lee Bates lived here, the center hall functioned as a lobby where her sister, Jeannie, oversaw the comings and goings of many visitors.

When I bought the house, each room on the first floor could be closed off with a door—so many doors! Closed off to conserve heat, perhaps, the doors allowed each room to be used publicly and privately—reading rooms, writing rooms, study halls. Neighbors recounted visiting Bates later in her life and playing games, with sweets always close by. I researched the history of the house at the Wellesley Historical Society, looking at the census records and city directories, and saw that from Bates's death in 1929 until the 1960s, the house was a boardinghouse, with as many as eleven unrelated adults living here, so each room was closed for privacy. I had taken some of the doors off their hinges so the first floor flows. The generous center hall leads out to the screened porch and backyard, people flowing too.

It seemed like the right idea to have our party in the backyard. I worked on getting the house ready. I wanted him to be proud of our beautiful home, I suppose. After the renovations the previous winter, the outside of the house was a mess. The dumpster, parked in front of the house for months, had killed the remaining pachysandra, and the grass was full of weeds. Some of the renovated areas were still unpainted. With the help of my neighbor Suzan and her crew, we got to work. The garden beds were edged, weeded, and mulched. Trees were trimmed, beds restructured, a path created. There was nothing to be done about the grass; frankly it should not exist in this shady yard on ledge outcroppings.

Suzan suggested replacing the pachysandra out front with a more beautiful ground cover. How Tommy hated "the fucking pachysandra," as he called it. I knew that if he were here we would tear it out and start over. But every time I looked at the damn stuff, all I could hear was him saying, "the fucking pachysandra," and decided to keep it. A greeting when I come up to the house every day, the fucking pachysandra.

By the time Saturday arrived, the house sparkled. A fresh coat of graphite paint on the back, new hydrangeas blooming, borrowed lawn furniture. My cousin Jonathan and his family had arrived on Thursday from Charlotte, North Carolina, so the rush of people was softened. Tommy's family had come over the previous night, so we had time to visit privately and warm up for the weekend. I could not be more grateful for the love of his sisters. He was their beloved baby brother; they felt a special kind of love and grief, and I felt a deep kinship with them.

By 3 p.m. people start arriving. Harry Connolly had gotten there early to set up a "Story Corps" room. A friend and colleague for fifteen years, he readily agreed to help tell the story of Tommy. Tommy's friends from New York, California, Connecticut, Rhode Island, and Sweden began to arrive. We captured three hours of stories on video while people lined up to participate.

His friend Eamon brought a cake, and we put it on a round table in the center of the hall. It read "Tommy Niles—the Whole Man" and featured a yin-yang design with half ocean beach and half city buildings. People arrived with coolers; we tapped the keg of Cisco brew. What exactly was going to happen was unclear. The barbeque arrived; people ate, drank, visited; the kids ran around and jumped on the trampoline.

And then my sister tells me it's time to cut the cake.

I didn't have a plan around this moment, or any other, for that matter. But here we were, living the only life we have. I had told Harry that I had prepared my vows and asked him if I should read them. He said, "No, it's too much." I said, "I'm going to do it."

At our engagement party the year before, Tommy had made a beautiful toast. Maybe I will write about that night another day, but at that event, his words had said it all. I often speak at public events, but in that most personal of spaces, I didn't need to say a thing.

But Tommy wasn't here. We would not be having a ceremony; we would not be exchanging vows in front of our friends and family. But I was here, and my love for him was here, so I grabbed my paper.

I stood on the patio, and my girls stood next to me, Bliss in the crook of my arm. The girls' friends were behind me, filling the corner of the patio. I said, "You only live once," and the teenagers chipped in, "YOLO!" "You got this, Mrs. Swenson." I wished I could have done it without crying, but that proved impossible. I may never have felt so naked in my whole life. Tears streamed down my face, and I heard Bliss crying next to me as I read.

Tommy, you were, and will always be, mine in love. I promise to honor the love that we shared, the life that we experienced together and the vision we shared for our future. I will always remember the feeling of your eyes meeting mine, your smile alighting on me. I will aspire to be the person I felt I was with you, and to continue to see myself through the lens of your adoration. I will celebrate the person that you were. I will remember your goodness, your passion, your sense of humor, your curiosity. I will represent you to our family, friends, and children as the extraordinary man that I knew and will strive to keep your memory alive for our children and grandchildren. I will carry you with me always, in my heart and in my soul. I will love you as long as I shall live.

Silence. There is no protocol for this, no polite ritual to fall back on. Andrew cleared his throat and took the plunge. Cool Canadian water. He said, "Let's make a toast to Katie." People raised their glasses, to Katie. More silence.

On the other side of the yard, Tara stepped a little higher up the hill on a ledge outcropping. She clinked her glass and everyone turned toward her, mercifully drawing attention away from me. Tommy and I had asked Tara to officiate our wedding. After a year of yoga class with her, we were inspired by her realness, honesty, humor, love of life—and her foul mouth. We experienced her together; she was ours together, our shared high priest-ess. We were not planning a church wedding, and we knew she would be the one to send us into our lives in the way that we wanted to go—fresh, serious, raw, joyous, ambitious, elevated.

Tara stood up taller on the rock, her red clogs giving her extra stature, her white dress flowing and her hair cascading regally out of her bun. She had been there the day Tommy died. She was there for us the whole time. After class, Tara and I were chatting in the yoga room as Tommy left the room to change his clothes, a normal day in every way.

She told her story to the group: How she met us, describing Tommy as this larger-than-life man, the beauty of him, the beauty of us, this giant and his bride-to-be. She talked about teaching, closing her eyes as she spoke, and started to move as she does in class, as if she were teaching through doing, stretching her body in the way that makes you work harder. You want to stretch more to get the divine feeling of blood rushing through your muscles, joints, synapses.

She spoke about opening her eyes one day in class and seeing that Tommy had come behind me, in tree pose, the pose I had told him was my favorite. Instead of doing his own tree on his mat, he came behind me and put his hands under my shoulder blades, urging me up. I lifted my hands into the air, looked up, and raised myself up on my toes, elevated fully in the highest expression of the pose, the highest expression of me. In hundreds of yoga classes, with thousands of people, she said she had never seen that before.

"He wasn't scared," she said; "I want you to know that he wasn't scared." As much as we cannot comprehend his death, we should know that in that moment he was not scared. She told a play-by-play of the day, which she had re-created to understand as fully as possible what had happened, with the help of her friend Caroline, who was there as a witness. Tommy was calm and in control. He was directing the EMTs by telling them what he was feeling. I was holding him. She told the group: "You must know this; he was not scared." And then he had crashed, losing consciousness. The EMTs used their paddles on him and he revived for a minute. He called out "Katie," and I said, "I'm right here with you, baby." And that was it. He never panicked. He was never alone. He was not scared. Somehow.

Then she continued. She spoke about me and what Tommy would want for me. She said I would love again, and that he would want that. It made me nervous as she was saying it, but also incredibly glad for her boldness and truth-telling. This is why we chose her. I understood what she was doing for me in that moment, rescuing me, giving me cover, taking me in, protecting me.

After the word of Tommy's death got out in the yoga community, there was fear, sadness, and some panic. Teachers responded in different ways. The most common response was surely the only right one—those who recognized that "but for the grace of God, he could have died after my class."

Tommy had gone to 167 classes that year, all hot, all hard, all different; his death had absolutely nothing to do with the class. He finished the class; he did his push-ups; he changed his clothes; he had a massive heart attack; he died. But while most teachers responded with empathy, a few did not. A tiny few blamed Tara, the studio, the class. Others responded with a sort of yogic bullshit. "She will have to stay strong in her center and allow the storm to rage around her. If she stays strong and grounded, it will die down." Holy shit.

When the tornado cuts a swath through a neighborhood and takes out the house of your neighbor, and your house is left standing, do you wish them well? Do you shout out your window to send them courage to withstand the wind and the rain, strength to keep their feet on the ground? I sure as hell hope not. I hope that you run out into the storm to drag them into your house. That you give them a blanket and a hot mug and run out and pick up their photo album that is out in the rain.

We rescue each other. That is what we do. When you are standing naked in your own backyard, reading your vows to your dead fiancé, you get to be rescued. When you strive to reach for the sky, balancing on one foot, you get to be held. When you feel the soul-crushing sadness of loss and experience profound trauma, you get to be cradled by your community. That is how Tommy did it. That is how we do it.

3

I Could Not Bear My Grief

but That I Must

JULY 26, 2017

Project People

I have always loved a project. This is in no way a project I would have chosen or predicted, but storytelling is clearly the project I need to do now. At my mother's office today, I saw a carpenter whom I have met a few times. I know his daughter-in-law, a wonderful and warm yoga teacher who is a new mother. I asked about her and the baby, and he showed me photos and video of his six-month-old granddaughter. But his other son had died three years ago. The pain was etched in his face. "I love to talk about him," he says, and I wished I had asked as much about that beloved lost son as about this beloved new baby.

Of course he wants to talk about him. That is all I want to do. Friends came over recently. We sat on the back porch and they brought wine and dinner. But they spoke about everything but Tommy. I felt ridiculous inserting at every turn, "Tommy thought . . ." "Tommy loved . . ." But at the same time, I thought, at least this summer, this week, this month, this year, we get to speak about him. I understand that in three years, I will still want to speak about him; in thirty years I will want to speak of him. Because the worst thing about losing the person you love once is losing him again and again. It's bad enough that he is gone from our daily lives. Can't he at least live on in our conversations and stories?

So, I write and write and write. I love writing because it allows me, forces me, to turn on my curious mind. Like somehow the act of remembering— the sorting, reliving, and learning—is itself a way to make him present in this moment. And I ask, I listen; I gather stories, tales, antics, photos.

I have a title for these memories: *In Bohemia: A Corona of Sonnets*, after Katharine Bates's poem. When every day feels like a day farther away from him, a day farther away from the activation of us, can you imagine how good it feels to make something? A project is a default, perhaps, an avoidance technique, a busyness strategy. But being a project person has its perks. At the end, you have something tangible. It could be a house, a renovation, a drawing, a website; there is an undeniable pleasure in both the process of making and the product completed.

Tommy loved a project too. He was a maker, doer, and builder. And this house, this Scarab and Bohemia within it, was one of our shared projects. So I get to work. I plan, think, sketch, research. I visited the Wellesley College Archives today, as if researching the house and its residents is a way to connect my past and present through the Scarab, this spatial envelope for all the lives within it. I started on the first archival folder. There are boxes ahead of me, waiting. I don't know what I will find there, but that is not the question. The search is everything; for now, the effort is all that is required.

There I found a poem, "The Debt," by Bates, today: "Because the years are few, I must be glad / Because the silence is so near, I sing." I'm excited, I have to say; there is pleasure in action, pleasure in production. Tommy felt that pleasure; he lived it, and so do I.

JULY 27, 2017
Right, Bodyguard?

"Right, bodyguard?" Tommy would say to me. In text messages he called me "BG" for short. Muhammad Ali was one of Tommy's many heroes. It's not hard to imagine how Tommy would have become captivated by "the greatest" athlete and man of his generation. Tommy was born in 1960, the year Ali won a gold medal at the Summer Olympics in Rome. He would have watched Ali through the 1960s—his upset of Sonny Liston, his name change from Cassius Clay to Muhammad Ali, his refusal to be drafted to Vietnam, giving up his titles, and the career peak that came later.

I find the black-and-white video on YouTube that Tommy used to recite by heart. An interviewer asks Ali, "Do you have a bodyguard?" Ali responds, "I have One bodyguard. He has no eyes though He sees. He has no ears though He hears. He remembers everything with the aid of mind and memory. When He wishes to create a thing, He just orders it to be and it comes into existence, but this order does not convey the words which takes the tongue to follow or the sound carrying ears. He hears the secrets of those under quiet thoughts. That's God Allah. He's my bodyguard. He's your bodyguard."

Tommy was enamored with this concept. His reflexive and rhetorical question to me was always, "Right, bodyguard?" For which there was only one answer: "Right, baby." What does it mean to really have someone's back, to be their bodyguard?

On May 18, I learned.

There was a beautiful young woman at the studio the day Tommy died. She had showered and was drying her hair after class, getting ready to head to work, just another day in her life. But then, Tommy was in crisis. There she was, first running with Tara to the street to meet the EMTs, then by my side, bewildered but steady. My witness to his last moments. What a trauma she experienced.

Later, riding back from the funeral home with my sister, where we had been preparing for the service, I felt mounting panic. I had to find her, I told Chrissie. Who was she? Was she okay? By the time we arrived home, there was a text message from her—a miracle of the digital age. It's almost impossible to describe the power of her intuitive connectedness, the utter beauty of her words, the depth of her insight. She witnessed the most profound moment of my life and reflected it back to me with more love than a person could imagine possible. All this from a stranger, an innocent bystander, a twenty-something woman filled with more courage and grace than most of us would dream of at any age.

Katie, it's caroline from hyp. i just got your number from tara, i hope that's ok. i haven't stopped thinking about you. the strength and composure you showed yesterday morning has gripped me and i haven't been able to apply words to do it justice. i know no amount of kind words or hugs can fill the gaping hole you must be feeling in your heart and soul. no pinch can wake you from the nightmare. but i hope you're finding comfort in friends and family and your girls—i'm sure they're just as strong and beautiful as you are. the love between you and tommy is palpable. not just yesterday morning where it was so clearly felt, but in all of the mornings you two came to tara's class together. i'm so sorry your true companion is no longer here—it's unimaginable—but i know he'll live on in your love and the legacy he's left behind. thinking of you always and here for anything. xo

There was nothing better than having Tommy Niles be my bodyguard. I got the chance to experience what it means to "have" someone—not in a possessive way, but in a way that holds the space for you, to be protected and confident in your ability to be your greatest self, a shield against detractors, be they internal or external. He taught me how to have one, and to be one.

Except that there are other bodyguards. Other witnesses. Other angels. There is Caroline in that moment, somehow able to shine the light of her beauty on the most profoundly wordless moment of your life. A person who was able to master her own emotional state so she could be fully present to another.

Maybe calling Caroline my bodyguard is too much. Or maybe it's just right. Maybe we can allow ourselves to be both our most spiritual beings and our most human selves. Maybe we can strive to protect each other here on earth. Right, bodyguard?

JULY 30, 2017

A Horseman with a Lance to Drive Away Evil Spirits

"There is nothing in the way of travel I have ever done so delightful as this voyaging on the Nile," wrote Katharine Lee Bates of her trip to Egypt. Bates traveled extensively, including her now-famous train trip across America with stops at Niagara Falls, the Chicago World's Fair, through the wheat fields of Kansas, and to Pikes Peak in Colorado Springs, which resulted in her verses for "America the Beautiful."

Her descriptions of the trip to Egypt were more intimate but no less powerful. "You must come," she wrote to her mother. "It's like nothing else under the sun. It's a land that cries with the strange voice of a ghost and yet the voice of our own inmost life—the land of that dust out of which human clay was made."

Bates moved into her new house in 1907, following her trip to Egypt. She brought home a small scarab of dull-green stone that she placed under the study mantel. When drawn as a hieroglyph, the scarab acquires a higher significance. It is the sign for the Egyptian verb meaning "become" or "create." In the hearth below the scarab she set a brick tile with an armored knight charging with his lance poised, warding off all cares and grief. Bates's niece, Dorothy Burgess, tells these stories and more in her book *Dream and Deed*, and I went looking for these hidden treasures with Harry. Harry has traveled the country with me for the past fifteen years, photographing the work of the Enterprise Rose Fellows, the architects we pair with community-based organizations. Harry and I have visited probably thirty-five states together—at the border of Mexico, in small and large cities, on Native American land, capturing the essence of communities working hard to build a future that reflects the strength and culture of their people.

This visit, Harry was up from Baltimore to photograph a fellowship event and took an interest in the Scarab. What happened to the stone that had been embedded in the mantel? The scarab itself is lost; it was removed from the mantel at some unknown time, by an unknown person, lost to history.

We did find the special knight tile in the brick hearth in the living room—we just needed a camera flash to see it. Harry used a photographer's trick to figure it out. He used the modeling light to show approximately what the flash will illuminate, then laid it on the ground, and the raking light brought out the shadows and revealed the horseman and lance. You still cannot see the imprint with the naked eye, but the photograph throws it into sharp relief.

Bates used the front living room as her study. She had a writing desk there and hosted seminars in the room before she moved up to Bohemia after Coman's death. We use it as our family living room—fireplace, no TV, gathering space for one, two, or twenty. For Christmas two years ago, I had given Tommy a beautiful backgammon set, and on nights when just the two of us were home, we'd light a fire and play.

One of my favorite nights in that room was in December of last year. My sister was having a big Christmas party, and Tommy and I invited two friends to join us. They were both single women, raising their kids on their own, one brand new to the single life, reinventing their lives.

We were dressed for the party, but first enjoying each other's company at home. Tommy's unassuming male energy gave sparkle to our evening. Our glasses were full, as he attended to us. He had all kinds of things in common with my newly single friend, and I watched her relax, laugh, veritably shine. Maybe this new life would be okay, I imagined her thinking, or perhaps only feeling. There was joy to be had; there was delight; there was sizzle and sparkle and beauty. With Tommy as our knight, we needn't fear.

AUGUST 3, 2017
"Ok darlin"

Some days it cuts too deep. How can reality feel so surreal, how can truth feel so unfair? Why are the facts so impossible to imagine? Some days I can accept that this is true. Tommy is gone and he's not coming back. Other days my mind cannot accept this. We cannot possibly have lost him.

Good mornin', sunshine. I relive Tuesday, May 16, again and again. If I can draw up all the details of that day, can I somehow rewind the tape of the last day of real reality? We skipped yoga that morning because Tommy had a big day at South Street Landing in Providence. On the river, he and his team were renovating the abandoned Narragansett Electric Plant for Brown University and the Rhode Island College School of Nursing. This complicated and intense project was nearly completed, and the historical and contemporary architecture merged to form a beautiful place. Various luminaries were visiting that day—perhaps the mayor or governor, the president of Brown University, the equity investors.

Tommy's morning followed a normal routine—making breakfast burritos and taking Bliss to school. We took the train to Boston together, where I stayed at my office and he went south for meetings and tours. The day passed quickly for both of us, and we didn't check in until about 4 p.m., when he sent me the first "tug" of the day from the train home, trying to get back for an appointment. We texted and then spoke. His phone battery was running low, and I sensed an unusual, low-grade panic in his voice. The train was stalled and making local stops; he would miss his appointment.

Plus, he had to get a big email out recounting the endless details of the project that were in his head, and seemingly in his head alone.

I caught the 5 p.m. train, and by the time I got home he was up in Bohemia, sitting in his favorite spot on the couch. I knew that when he got home, he'd have said hello to Bliss and gone upstairs to change into jeans and take off his shoes. He'd sit on the couch, pick up his guitar, and play a bit, letting the stress of the day go. He'd lie down on the gray leather, feet up, his happy place, facing west, and doze for ten minutes. By the time I got home he was back at it, plugging away at the email.

Kiss.

He had a way to go on the epic memo, so I headed down to start dinner. I returned twice to send an email from my computer, my workday also not quite done. But I am also aware that I made the trip up the stairs just to be near him as he worked. I am at my desk, and he is on his laptop on the couch, each of us at home in our places.

Peace.

I finished dinner prep and went to get Bliss at lacrosse, chatting with parents at the field, a pretty night. He finished his work, came downstairs, and texted me, "Are you picking up Bliss?" Yes. Liv home, he said. Great, finish the dressing and we'll eat as soon as we get home.

"Ok darlin."

By the time Bliss and I walked in, domestic bliss was in place, the workday chaos receded. Dinner, the four of us, happy banter, good food. The girls started clearing the dishes. We got that, we said; go, get your work done. They scampered off quickly before the offer could be rescinded. I remember actively wanting to do the dishes with him, needing that time alone with him at the end of the day, to knit us back into our order.

I can't remember what we ate. I can't remember what we talked about. I can't remember what happened between dinner and bed, except the feeling: quiet, calm, safe, happy.

"Ok darlin," was his last text to me. How can that possibly be true? How can such sweetness turn to sorrow overnight? How can the most normal day of my life be a Tuesday in the past, and not some future day, not today?

AUGUST 4, 2017
I Believe in Katie Swenson

In my optimistic mind, we had a wedding and a honeymoon. Right after we got engaged, my sister offered to throw an engagement party. Gather thirty or so people at her house, locals only. Somehow the guest list rapidly expanded, and my mom ordered a tent. It was a beautiful night and nearly a hundred people showed up. Our kids and many of our friends were there, but no out-of-town guests. My friend Sue Ann walked in with a bouquet, which I carried all night, instantly transformed into a bride. I said that night that had my father been present, we would have just gotten married on the spot!

Tommy made a toast. I wish I had a recording of it now. My sister recalls first and foremost that he said, "I may or may not believe in a God, but I believe in Katie Swenson." The women swooned. A friend later remarked that I had said nothing publicly that night. What was there for me to say? Tommy said it all for us.

Later, my nephew's friend who was there sent me a note about the night:

> Tommy spoke with a subtle inkling of a man who had perhaps previously grown close to losing hope of ever finding the love that he so yearned for. Any despair that might have been previously was dissipated completely when Katie entered his life. The way that he looked at her from that porch said more than any of the words that followed. In Katie, he had found everything he'd ever dreamed of. He praised her for all that made her so beautiful and talented, well-respected, and strong. The gorgeous woman he'd observed in early morning yoga turned out to be so much more as he'd began to fall in love with her. He stood there that night and whether he said it or not, it was clear that with Katie by his side, there could not be a happier man in the world as far as he was concerned.

AUGUST 6, 2017
Sleeping Porch

When we were planning Tommy's move into this house full of women, we debated the options. He had already been staying here for the past year, but he treaded carefully, making sure to give the girls their privacy. A few years ago, I had turned my room—originally Katharine Lee Bates's room—into a master suite with its own bath and one closet. Tommy and I pared down our wardrobes and were perfectly comfortable there, in the summer especially, with the door open to a sleeping porch—a screened room on the southeast side of the house where the morning sun streams in and afternoons are nice and shady. Over the years, the girls and I had tried different furnishings and for many summers even moved a twin bed out there, where Liv slept. It became her haven. By some sibling roulette, Liv had had first choice of rooms when we moved here. This was the room she really wanted, but she also knew it was meant to be the master, so she had ceded it to me. But the porch was always hers. She would disappear there for hours with a book. Two summers ago we hung a hammock, perfect for reading and sleeping.

Tommy and I decided we would move upstairs, even before the plans were made for this magical place. Liv, then sixteen, would finally get the room with the sleeping porch, a retreat perfect for her last years of high school. Tommy always felt natural in this house full of women, perhaps because of growing up with his mom and sisters. He brought his curious mind to the household dynamics. Before he died, he was working on patching and painting the closet in Sophie's room. It never got finished, but magically, Bliss's hooks were back up on her wall, having been pulled out by heavy backpacks. I saw it and wondered, When did he get that done? A small parting gift. He'd become so thoroughly necessary to our lives. Sophie said, "Mom, we did it all ourselves before; you know we can do this."

This house does perfectly well as a house of women, for women. But frankly, it did well to have a man around too, as did we.

AUGUST 7, 2017
First Edition

A present arrives in the mail from my high school friend Emily, a first edition of *Yellow Clover*, the most beautiful of gifts. The card alone is wonderful, expressing her faith in me, in life, in the beauty and heartbreak. She is right that I already owned a copy of *Yellow Clover*, but none with the elegance of a first edition, nor with its own story written into it. In this first edition, a newspaper article is embedded in the first page that, over time, created a sort of latter-day palimpsest, framing the signature of its original owner, Lilly Prentiss Case from Chicago—an intaglio for the inscription of name, date, location—the essential ingredients for the beginning to any story.

A little over ten years ago, I had received a similar gift. It was also a dark and confusing time in my life. I was getting divorced and moving "home" to Wellesley in an attempt to regain equilibrium. We had been incredibly happy in Charlottesville, Virginia. I got my master of architecture degree at the University of Virginia, and we loved the town and stayed for almost a dozen years. All three girls were born there, and it was very much our home. But divorce is a brutal and disruptive shock, and ours was certainly painful. I had decided that the best thing for me and the girls was to regroup near our extended family outside Boston.

The problem was that as a teenager I had vowed I would never live in Wellesley again. I saw Wellesley only as a banker's suburb—the executives commuting to Boston with wives and children at home. White. Homogeneous. Conservative. My return mostly felt like failure. I was coming back, but on my knees. Divorced, single mom, traveling for work, needing support, it felt like I was crawling home. I had come to Wellesley on a rainy April weekend to look for a house. My mom's best friend, Sandy, reminded her that the house of Katharine Lee Bates was still on the market. I should see it.

The Scarab had been vacant for three years. Following the death of his wife, Muriel, Walter Robinson had died in 2004, leaving the house to a trust. They had purchased the house in 1960 and made many changes.

By the time I saw it in 2007, it had endured forty-three years of "improvements." I was hesitant. I love houses, I love old houses, and I love a project, but I was tired. I was alone, and I had lost everything. How would I do it? My mom bolstered me morally and financially. "You can do this." We put in a lowball offer and it was accepted.

I returned to Charlottesville to tell the kids, put our house on the market, and start our goodbyes. Those were very sad times. But then my friend Robin gave me a gift. A book. *Dream and Deed: The Story of Katharine Lee Bates* by Dorothy Burgess. It was a revelation. Robin's sticky tabs every place in the book where the Scarab is mentioned marked a path forward for me. It is one of my prized possessions to this day. This book, written with firsthand experience, opened up an entirely different view of Wellesley: intellectual, feminist, liberal.

I started to see a Wellesley that was one of the catalytic birthplaces of women's education. I loved reading about the formation of Wellesley College, with architecture and landscape architecture intimately woven with its mission. I especially loved reading about this house and these women—about their passion for poetry, history, social justice, travel, and their salons and classes in the house. The more I read about these two Katies and their house, the more I started to paint a picture in which I could thrive in Wellesley—a new version of what Wellesley could be, different than my experience growing up. I would discover, and continue to discover, the stories of these women, this house, this town, this college, but that book flipped a switch for me. I could make a new mental construct, create a different story, and it was a lifesaver.

I'm so grateful to have the kind of friends that spark you along the way, to sometimes push you, read your writing, soothe your soul, show another path. To send you a signed first edition with a beautiful note. To have the pleasure of reading these sonnets of love and grief on original paper, with real type, the edition that Bates held, smooth softcover and ribbon band of yellow clover.

My River

My neighbor Catherine has a talent. She sees things; she has visions that most of us don't have. I am sure that is off-putting to some people, but I have always welcomed her perspective. Before I met Tommy, she asked me about a man with whom I'd had a few dates. "He is not your river," she said, "and I see you as a river, running over, around, and through rocks, polishing them, as you flow to the ocean." Tommy was my river. Or maybe I was the river for him; I am not sure how the metaphor plays out. But what I know was the feeling. I felt like we flowed in and around each other, moving forward, making progress, and softening rough edges. We filled in the space; obstacles just got polished or smoothed away.

Now with him gone, I feel those rough edges. Time is passing, and presumably I am supposed to be getting back to normal, getting back to work, getting out. But I encounter many barriers. Sometimes it is the shock of grief that stalls me. Other times it is a more existential threat. I allow myself the self-indulgence to feel sorry for myself, or sorry for the kids, or just so terribly sorry that he is gone. I get caught up in it all not making sense. The world was so much better with him than without him, not just for me, but for so many, so how could this reality possibly be true? Another version is a sort of paralysis. The flow has stopped; there is no momentum, no tide, and no particular will to make things advance. A stasis. A future without him—is it worth it after all? Treading water is all I can do.

Catherine has a new vision. "I had a dream that you were swimming in a pool of water, full of stars, opalescent, and the stars were in the water. You were swimming by yourself and you ducked your head underwater, and I felt the cold, clear water against your skin; it felt so good. The salt water was also buoying you, supporting you. When you came out on the beach, there were already footprints there, and they too were starry. As you walked up to your towel or spot, the footprints that predated you were disappearing. There was a note written in the sand, 'Be careful when you swim, Love.' It was not a warning; it was sweet, the way you might speak to a child: 'Take your raincoat.' It meant that you have a sense that you are being watched over, that you are still the focus of Tommy's life and that he is still watching out for you. He is saying to you, 'I can't watch you all the time, so please try to be cautious and be safe while you are having fun.'"

Oh, God, I hope he is watching out for us. We all needed him so much. I hope he is watching out for the boys, for the girls, for me. I'd love to feel that in my life. But that seems like it is expecting a lot.

Instead, I know that I have to be the person I am, or that I was, at my best with him. I try to imagine his insight, predict his thoughts, but it's hard to have a two-way dialogue by yourself. Just a fact.

And, I don't have enough data points on grief and death and loss. He had his share, to be sure: His father at age twelve. His mother in his thirties, and then his best friend, Andy McDonald, in his early fifties. He may have been too young to fully experience his father's death, but I know that his mother's death hit him hard, and I heard about the journey to Elmira for her funeral, a poem he wrote for her and read at her service. And also that life was so busy and he felt like he did not make the space to properly grieve his beloved mom.

I heard the story of Andy's death. He entered into the fight against cancer with Tommy Niles as his wingman (Right, bodyguard?). I have the heavy-duty juicer to show for it. Tommy juiced and juiced for Andy, and I am sure he did whatever else they thought might get him through his cancer. But Andy died, and Tommy told me about the funeral. A chair that Andy had reclaimed from the town dump was repositioned as a throne on the altar. When Andy's girlfriend arrived, there was a pause: Where would she sit? Tommy saw a young recruit in uniform and instantly recognized him as a good man with a good-soldier code of conduct. He asked him to usher "the girlfriend" with regal respect to her place of honor at Andy's service. I know that as the friend and griever, Tommy wanted to make it okay for everyone else. But he also grieved.

What would he say to me now? Would he say, "Feel it all; let it rip through you" or "Write until you can't write any longer"? Or would he say, "Have faith; know that I love you and I am here for you; you cannot see me or hear more, but have faith that I am here watching over you; feel okay, feel held, feel loved and not alone"? Or would he say, "I am sorry that this sucks so much for you; believe me, this is the very last thing I wanted, but here you are, so you have to make the most of it. Buckle down, get to the business of living, of the kids' lives, your work life, take refuge in that life and let the pain dissipate slowly over time"? Or would he say, "Start juicing and don't stop until the world is free of cancer and heart disease and stops taking beautiful men and women, too young, unfairly"?

I can't write his script on this one, and it is in this that I feel most alone. Your man—your person—is so essential. On the domestic front, the kids' front, the social front, the intimate front, he / she is your go-to guide, back-board, problem-solving conversation for all the life events, no matter how mundane or existential—the stuff you simply cannot discuss with anyone else. As time passes, these questions and conversations loom larger; time creates pent-up demand to thoroughly address life's complexity together; you need him more over time, not less. It's gotten too complicated, and the experience is more than I can interpolate on my own.

AUGUST 10, 2017
Art Wall

Do I tell this story from the beginning or the end? I guess it all ends up in the same place, so I'll start from the end, which maybe is also the beginning. I was looking at photos on Tommy's iPhone feed last night and came across cropped close-ups of five figures. Years ago, I had given my mom a piece of art, black ink on paper, that hangs in her back hall. The artist, Ben Schonzeit, is a lifelong friend. When I was living in SoHo in the early 1990s and trying to make it as a modern dancer, I inherited an aerobics gig from a friend. Tuesday nights, I taught a class to artists in one of their lofts on Greene Street. There were four regulars—three women and one man, Ben. Over those years of aerobics, we became friends. I have a framed watercolor painting that he did of me in 1993, which Tommy hung over his new sink in Bohemia. "KT at 25," Ben wrote, and I am there, sketched in sailor pants and striped shirt, midriff showing and sinuous, muscular arms, a beret. Tommy loved this sketch, but he loved the ink drawings at my parents' house even more.

Tommy loved my body. He loved it in motion, he loved it still. On his phone are dozens of photos of me, many from the back or side, taken without my knowing. He loved being near me in yoga class, where I could really move. With his nearsightedness, he wanted to be next to me—the only person in focus in the room. But Tommy saw me in all these dancing and moving figures.

I brought Tommy to Ben's New York studio while Bohemia was under construction—to get Ben's approval, I suppose, and have Tommy meet the artist of his favorite pieces.

I had been in the city for work, and we stayed at the Aloft in Brooklyn. We met friends for dinner in Tribeca and rode Citi Bikes home over the Brooklyn Bridge. It was my bridge, in his view, forever captured by a photo of me taken when I was twenty-five, in black and white, leaping on the bridge at dawn on a gray day, a man walking solo behind me. My roommate at the time was a fashion photographer's assistant; we went out that morning and I jumped and jumped while he captured this majestic image.

Tommy got up early the next morning and took himself on his own trip down memory lane, to the Brooklyn waterfront and the escapades of his youth. We went back to the city midmorning and had coffee and breakfast at Café Gitane before walking through Little Italy to Ben's studio on Mercer Street in SoHo.

There are a few artists left in SoHo, and Ben is one, thank God. He's lived and worked in this loft since the 1970s. The living space is spare and modest, but the studio has the soaring ceilings and windows you crave in such a space, and ample room for production. Ben has another studio in the country where the heavy lifting and big sculpture happens, but the painting, collages, and smaller sculptures are made here.

Ben was working on a series of collages when we visited. Figures—dancing figures, all movement and gesture, made of scraps of paper and found objects. There is a ledger, a cobbler's bookkeeping record, in the background of many of the figures. There is a story in each, a character, a spirit. And there are a lot of them; Ben is one of the most prolific producers I know. He seems to be constantly making, and he was spinning out both sculptural collages and paper collages, hundreds of them.

The large wall of Ben's studio is itself a work of art. Constantly changing, it's a display wall but also a working wall. When big buyers come, I am sure he makes conscious decisions about what to hang, but when we were there, the wall showed his work in progress, an exploration of movement and collage.

Our visit prompted three takeaways. First, Tommy became even more certain that all the figures were variations on me, studies in movement and choreography. Delight in physical form, he said, joy in motion.

Second, we started talking about making our own art wall and how we would design Bohemia. The space was being demolished but our rebuilding plans were still in progress. We started arranging the space to have an art wall that could be a constantly evolving creative display. All of Bohemia's other surfaces, including the richly varied ceiling, were clad in wood, but we would drywall a 10-by-20-foot wall with lighting for displaying exhibitions or projects.

The day we moved in, we hung our first attempts—letters spelling out B O H E M I A on cool clips I brought home from Magazine Street in New Orleans, along with old maps and found objects. Later, the wall morphed into a project wall and I started to use it for research. I drew the timeline of the Scarab and the Katharines on the wall, starting with Nathaniel Hawthorne in the 1840s, Bates's and Coman's births in 1859 and 1857, the founding of Wellesley College, and their careers, lives, deaths, and onward, tracing the house to the present time. Tommy also set up a projector to screen on the wall; he loved making videos and dreamed of future projects. We watched the Patriots win the Super Bowl on a crystal-clear, 8-by-10-foot screen, and the last season of *Peaky Blinders* in living color.

We worked on our shared projects there too. We diagrammed the wedding and the life decisions we were making. A chart with Money / Health Insurance / Life Insurance / Tuition / Legal—all the things we were working on to make our partnership complete. It's hard to look at that now, these plans, intentions, all revolving around a July 22 wedding.

The week after his death, the wall changed again. The boys and the girls and I met in Bohemia to plan the funeral. We gathered in front of the art wall and "charretted" the service, letting the ideas emerge, putting up speaker names, songs, and written passages. My handwriting was too messy for Bliss, so she took over with index cards and we moved things around together until everything found its spot. It was an integrated project design process. A proponent of "lean design" at work, Tommy would have been proud of the process, and exceptionally proud of the product. The seven of us came together to understand how to honor his spirit; we did it collaboratively and creatively, and it showed. People said to me later that they have never been to such a memorial.

But back to Ben's paintings and the third takeaway from our visit. Tommy died on May 17, but his birthday was right around the corner on May 25. Birthdays meant a lot to him—his own and others'. It is probably not a surprise that he saw birthdays as a chance to celebrate the person, and he loved to do that. We wanted nothing more than to celebrate this man, our hero, our loving prince. And this year would be a particularly big year, since we would be married in just a few months. I had been planning.

I went to New York on May 15 for work and then to execute my plan. I got to Ben's studio around 7:30 p.m., after an affordable-housing roundtable in Tribeca. Ben and Miriam invited me to stay for dinner, and after we finished, we went into the studio to select some prints of the collages.

I decided that I would choose eight. Eight of us in our new family, the family of our dreams. Eight figures, each in his or her own dance, able to be put together into many variations or stand alone as single figures, each its own work of art. The one with the black background is Popeye—that's Ben. But in my mind that figure was also Tommy, the father figure, eating his spinach and trying to make everything okay while the world and its people spin around him, colorful and dancing to their own rhythm. I debated my choices, but I didn't have too long to decide because I had to catch a flight home that night. Ben would sign the prints, and his assistant would send them in the mail in time for the 25th. They arrived on May 20. Tommy was dead and would never see them.

Except that, of course, they are his. He loves them / would have loved them, however one says this. I know it without having to question it. I wanted to open them on his birthday with all the kids, since they are them too, but by the time the 25th came, two days after the memorial service, everyone was spent. The family of our dreams was fractured, hurting. I opened the box and hung them, using clips and pushpins at first, to test out the spacing.

They are perfect. Bohemia did not feel incomplete without them, but now the space really sings (or dances). I am having them framed to let them soar, and they will become a more or less permanent installation on the art wall. Bohemia will still be filled with people, despite going from two to one so quickly and completely. It will still be the backdrop for joy in motion.

AUGUST 17, 2017
The Year of Magical Thinking

I cried on the plane. I started writing and then I started sobbing, as I often do—tears and mucus streaming, but not loud, barely a sound. I had the whole row to myself during the seven-hour flight from Amsterdam to Kigali. I felt alone in the back of the plane, away from the world.

"A gift from us, to help you write your memories." The flight attendant hands me a beautiful journal with handmade paper and off-white pages, closed with a button and elasticized string. His hand is large and presses on my upper arm, as if he is unafraid to touch me. He is unafraid to give me a close look, right in the eye, despite the tears and my head lowered. A frank and present human interaction. This KLM leg of the journey has mostly Dutch staff; they are more present than the Americans, and kinder. The tall one (bald) is not the only one. It's not a fluke. The other one, with black wavy hair, slightly receding hairline, handsome like an Italian actor, squats down every time he comes my way. He was the one who insisted on an answer. Not content to leave me to my tears, not content with "Are you okay?" He had to know what was wrong. "I lost my husband," I say, the easiest summary. Ahhh. Do they know, somehow, what that means?

I am reading Joan Didion's *The Year of Magical Thinking*. She says there was a time in America when death was close and a part of life; we understood it and had protocol in place. She cites a chapter from Emily Post on how to help the griever. It is long, involved, astutely accurate from my experience of the complete physiological disruption, the physicality of the experience of being out of body. She offers practical remedies: sunshine, hot tea to help the griever. "The cook may suggest something that appeals to their taste—but very little should be offered at a time, for although the stomach will be empty, the palate rejects the thought of food, and digestion is never in best order."

A new friend, a widow, has invited me into her private Facebook group. They call it The Club No One Wants to Join, Teton Chapter. One member laments, "No one wants to hear about it. I post some happy-memory pictures of my husband, but nothing morbid." Oh my, the rules I have broken. I have shared my grief online, shared the rawness of it, shared Tommy's death, his beauty and his heartbreak. "That stuff does not belong on Facebook," I hear. "Facebook is for smiling photos, kids, and kittens." Fair enough. I stop posting. With respect for the now-ancient wisdom of Emily Post, Didion continues that as death itself has become removed—it happens in hospitals now in the US, not at home—"the pressure of a new 'ethical imperative to enjoy oneself,' a novel 'imperative to do nothing that might diminish the enjoyment of others,' has forced grief and grievers to go underground." She continues: "Grief turns out to be a place none of us know until we reach it . . . We don't expect this shock to be obliterative, dislocating to both body and mind. We might expect that we will be prostrate, inconsolable, crazy with loss. We do not expect to be literally crazy, cool customers who believe that their husband is about to return and need his shoes . . . Nor can we know ahead of the fact (and here lies the heart of the difference between grief as we imagine it and grief as it is) the unending absence that follows, the void, the very opposite of meaning, the relentless succession of moments during which we will confront the experience of meaninglessness itself."

Keep me in the darkness of this plane, this world where there is a greater density of people than one encounters in everyday life, but where the rules around social engagement are rigid, at least on American flights. Be polite, but don't be forward. Take up as little space as possible. Don't snore. I can sit and sob in the dark.

AUGUST 19, 2017
Being Mortal

Being in Rwanda takes me right back to New Zealand, the first big trip Tommy and I took together last March. It takes me forward too, no mistake, but going back and going forward are hand in hand these days. This has been a summer of tremendous sadness, overwhelming loss, of just plain missing Tommy so much it aches. But it's also been an incredible summer with the girls—a summer of closeness, discovery, creativity, and meaning.

And so, it happens that I am visiting Sophie in Rwanda—my first trip to Africa. I have thought about coming here since 2010, when I met Michael Murphy and the architecture firm he cofounded, MASS Design Group, one of the most exciting firms in architecture today. Founded in Rwanda, MASS has built hospitals, schools, universities, and housing there, throughout Africa, and around the world. An important US project is under construction—the National Memorial for Peace and Justice in Montgomery, Alabama—a stunning memorial to commemorate the victims of lynching, which forces us to confront racial terrorism and its ongoing effects.

It wasn't until now that I understood I could do this. I hadn't expected to find Tommy in Africa, but of course he is here. He would absolutely love it here, and I feel him here so clearly. I think back to Tommy and me in New Zealand, starting the day in rainy Christchurch, determined to follow the sun, driving through the rainforest and Arthur's Pass, emerging to sunshine on the west coast of the South Island. We arrived at Hokitika, this amazing beach on a peninsula where the fresh water of the Hokitika River meets the salty Tasman Sea. The sunshine and clear skies mean that Mt. Cook (over 12,000 feet!) and the Southern Alps are in clear view behind us. Tommy, spellbound, almost childish, is beside himself. He skips rocks, he throws sticks, he runs into the ocean. What a trip, what a moment, what a world.

I had a sense of what life with Tommy would have been like. Life without Tommy is less clear, yet it holds its own possibilities. Here I am on another continent, my second time out of the US this year, and I am thinking perhaps not my last.

Sophie changed her summer plans, radically, in May after Tommy's death. "Tommy was too amazing a person to not have him affect you fully," she says. She pivots. A second year in a cubicle in downtown Boston has lost whatever allure it had—the paycheck, the resume. That was last year, and this year could not be more different; she learned her lesson from Tommy and she's ready to live it. So was I, or at least I was ready to help her do that. I introduced her to MASS Design Group and she did the rest. A month in the Boston office, a month in the Kigali office, working on the Rwanda Institute for Conservation Agriculture. She was off to Africa alone, just like that, twenty years old and fearless.

I see the girls doing it; can I do it too? What if I think of all the things that seemed so possible with him, pending, right there for the doing, and do them anyway? What if I could learn his lesson so completely and act on it, like they are doing? I need time. I'm too sad, too scared to do it alone. "What is it that we need in order to feel that life is worthwhile?" I read that question somewhere over the summer but cannot remember who asked it. It's fair to say that we can be capable and independent but also that needing each other, loving each other, does make life worthwhile.

My widow friend's husband died eleven years ago. He was a great outdoorsman and extreme skier. He died on the mountain, which she avoided for years after his death. As her grief started to soften, she started a foundation in his name. Through the foundation, she now brings local kids, mostly children of immigrants, skiing and hiking. She loved her husband and misses him every day, but now, she says, she wouldn't trade. If she could magically have him back but give up those kids? No way. Loving a person deeply is meaningful, and at this moment I would choose to have Tommy back. But maybe over time, you come to realize that for life to be worthwhile, you need to have loving relations of all kinds, loving relations that allow you to get outside yourself, outside Bohemia, and move forward.

4

Do You Remember

Still Your

Dear-Loved Earth?

AUGUST 21, 2017

Vulnerability Is Our Most Accurate Measure of Courage

The day after our first date, I asked Tommy to have coffee with me. I felt instantly comfortable with him and energized at the same time. I wanted to see him again, to make sure that what I was feeling was real. I would be leaving for a week the following day, so I suggested a coffee.

He got there first. He was nervous, as was I. He had something to tell me and wanted to get it off his chest, to let me know some essential truth or fact, to clear it off the table. Did he think I'd run away? His honesty surprised me, and while it was not at all difficult to listen to him and accept his "admission," I had no idea how to respond with an example of my own. I hadn't prepared for such vulnerability so soon.

The coffee date went well—an understatement. It sealed us, I think, as the real deal. He asked to pick me up from work and drive me home later that day, the first of many commutes together. As we sat in traffic on the Mass Pike hours later, I was ready to share more with him. I remember this sense of relief. No posturing, only honesty and acceptance.

He saved the note I sent him later that night on his phone, which I later found in his notes:

Thanks for a super nice, and sort of surprising day. Appreciate you making room, it was really nice to have a chance to spend some time together. I was thinking tonight about what I would possibly tell you if I revealed one salient truth and decided I honestly wouldn't know where to begin. Emotionally scarred, jagged edged, confident insecure, mama bear take no prisoners, hippy chick emotive girl-woman looking to find sexy secure intuitive analytical stable kind adventurist with big ideas and simple desires.

Heaven help us.

I like it that you sort of "get" me in a way, abstract though that might be, and are both quasi impressed and also nonplussed. That's a relaxing zone for me. And you are super cute.

Have a great weekend,

Katie

I don't have the response, or any other texts from those earliest days, but I love reading this immediate capture. First, of course, I couldn't have described him better after knowing him for years: "sexy secure intuitive analytical stable kind adventurist with big ideas and simple desires." What strikes me most was his immediate instinct to invite me into vulnerability with him—on day two. What he revealed was not shocking, just a man with a broken heart who stayed open to love even through disappointment. We are not the sum of our actions, or our past, we who have divorced; it does not mean that we are unfit for marriage.

Tommy sent me a TED talk on vulnerability by Brene Brown. He first watched it in 2014 before we met. Brown says, "Vulnerability is not weakness. I define vulnerability as emotional risk, exposure, uncertainty. It fuels our daily lives. And I've come to the belief—this is my twelfth year doing this research—that vulnerability is our most accurate measurement of courage. To be vulnerable, to let ourselves be seen, to be honest."

Brown connects resisting vulnerability with shame and the desire to hide our weaknesses. Empathy, she posits, is the antidote to shame. If we are really going to find our way back to each other, we need to be able to make a safe space to hold each other and just listen. She says: "You show me a woman who can actually sit with a man in real vulnerability and fear, I'll show you a woman who's done incredible work. You show me a man who can sit with a woman who's just had it, she can't do it all anymore, and his first response is not 'I unloaded the dishwasher!' But he really listens—because that's all we need—I'll show you a guy who's done a lot of work."

Tommy Niles had done a lot of work. He loaded and unloaded the dishwasher, but more important, he listened. I'm unbelievably sad that I did not have more time with him, but I am so glad that I met him when I did, at this incredible moment in his own life when he had been deep in his own work, understanding relationships, courage, empathy, sympathy, self-respect, and vulnerability. Vulnerability regulated the rhythm of our relationship, and there was nothing we couldn't talk about. Slowly, with a pause, no judgment, letting the conversation unfold. Listening, responding, loving.

AUGUST 22, 2017
Architecture

There were a lot of calls to make. I knew most of Tommy's colleagues, but some I had only heard of, like Paul Gorman from the South Shore YMCA. Tommy's undergraduate degree was in engineering, and he had dedicated his professional life to design and development. Tommy had worked for years with CV Properties, on work ranging from hotels to office and university buildings. He loved buildings, he loved the act of building, and he loved builders. But mostly he loved the people on the team.

Tommy also did side work as both as a consultant and a volunteer, and the South Shore YMCA was one of Tommy's favorite projects. He had been hired as a consultant to help build a new Y in Quincy, now the largest Y in the Northeast. The boys and I decided to direct donations in Tommy's name to the Y.

Paul was shocked by the news of Tommy's death. Tommy had been scheduled to meet with someone on the team that fateful Wednesday morning, and he hadn't shown up. I called Paul the day after his death to confirm that he would set up a donation page and make sure we had the obituary language right, and I had to break the news.

I found Paul's perspective so insightful. If you knew Tommy, you would have heard him rave about the Y, but you may not have known that Tommy led the project management over what would become a six-year period—three years on contract and three more years as a volunteer. Numerous times, Paul had offered to pay him for what was essentially a real job, but Tommy didn't accept. Paul described Tommy's unique ability to see the big-picture vision and manage the most-minute details in service of that vision. He also had the ability to keep the details in his head, making him the one person who really knew everything about the project.

The Quincy YMCA now has a membership twice what was projected, and reflects Quincy's diverse population. Paul says its welcoming inclusiveness is proof of the building's success. I think that's what architects do. They understand that a building is a means to achieve a mission, and the design and details make that mission a success.

A month after Tommy died, I went down to Providence with Sue Ann to visit his project. We parked outside the South Street Power Station and Narragansett Electric Lighting Company Plant, where his company was still working. No one stopped us as we walked through the building. It is gorgeous, an absolute stunner. A number of developers had given up on the project because it was so difficult and complex. But wow, what a thing to leave behind. The day before Tommy died, he took a "money shot" of the building from across the bridge. I'm glad that he felt pride that day, even amid the pressure.

It wasn't until I saw Fernando's crew working in the lobby that I really lost it. I saw Leon first. He had been one of the first at our house when we started demolition in Bohemia, and he was one of the last on final cleanup. These wonderful men who so beautifully crafted our house in its domestic scale were working in this soaring industrial castle, with steel stairs floating through the 90-foot-high brick space where the turbine used to be. God, how I miss them. I wish those guys could come back for one more Saturday breakfast, family style.

But no wonder they made the trip from Providence to Wellesley. Tommy put people first. When we met and he was building the hotels in the middle of that epic Boston winter, he was also helping to teach a class at Northeastern University and brought students out on-site. "When you draw that detail," he would say, "imagine what it's like to be the guy in the field making that connection, that weld, at 10 degrees in the snow after working outside for hours. Think about how his hands work, his tools. Your details are never just lines on a page; they should always be about how the person will read those drawings and make that connection in real time."

I miss talking shop with him. I learned so much. I have the urge to go back one day and see if I can find all the projects Tommy worked on. To make a list or catalog that captures those places he made, from Boston to Los Angeles and San Francisco. But I know that the buildings were only the vehicle for him. That it was the process of building and the people involved that interested him most, and the human stories of those buildings are harder to re-create than the list of built artifacts.

AUGUST 23, 2017

Sunshine (i.e., There Is an Us)

In the notes section on his phone, Tommy saved a message I sent him on our second day together, adding lyrics from the song "Sunshine" by Mike Doughty. The lyrics were slightly off, either what he heard or what he wanted to hear. "She's not a lush, she's a juniper enthusiast / Hippie-assed, friend of the grooviest." We must have listened to that song on that first commute together. Music, always music. We had a broad range of shared music, and then so much new. We had more overlap than I would imagine in 1980s and '90s "alternative" and punk. He loved blues and gospel. We'd share songs, listen in the car together for hours, make play lists. For Christmas last year we gave each other record players and a few records. In fact, we exchanged a few of the same records—*Blue* by Joni Mitchell and *After the Gold Rush* by Neil Young. The girls couldn't believe it. They laughed, in awe, I think, saying to each other, "If we didn't know they were perfect for each other, we do now." He was playing Eddie Vedder, Neil Young, and the Beatles on his guitar before he died, but he recorded other songs. Thank goodness we have those recordings, but we must be prepared to cry when we listen to them. I love listening to "Sunshine" over and over, but Bliss can't listen anymore; it makes her too sad.

Easter of our first year, just a month into our relationship, I went to early yoga. When I got out of class, I walked to my car, got in, and looked behind me to get out of my parallel parking space. On the back windshield, written so that it could be read in the mirror, were the words from "Sunshine": "there is an us." "I wrote a mash note, it said "there is an us" / I wrote it on your car in the windshield dust." It is faded now, but when the sunlight hits the glass of the rear window, I can see it still, forever impressed into the surface.

That was a hard morning. He had gotten us Peet's coffee and walked up with it to my car window. I got in his car with him and we drove around aimlessly, just talking. I was headed to church later and then to my parents' house with the kids and extended family for an Easter egg hunt and dinner. He was not sure what he would do. I hadn't introduced him to my family yet, so inviting him to Easter dinner was obviously premature, but in that moment, all I wanted to do was to scoop him up and bring him home.

I can't remember the details of our conversation in the car, but I can remember the mood, the feeling, the tension of that time, the vulnerability and openness, the fear and the commitment. It was a defining moment: "there is an us."

He hid the eggs at my parents' house while we were at church, worried that he would be seen as an intruder. Although we were just an "us" at that point, the circle of "us" was already clear: there would be no us without the larger us. He might not yet come to dinner, but he sure as hell was going to be the one to hide the eggs.

> I want to go where you are
> Send you my ghost in a mayonnaise jar
> For real, yeah, for real, for real
> I'd give you every charm that I know how to steal
> I could be the speaker for your microphone
> We could get together on the memory foam
> The only here is here
> Dark is dissipating like a bad idea
> We got everything but time

I ended an early writing with those "Sunshine" lyrics that turned out to summarize our relationship: "We got everything but time." Did we somehow know? When I read the hundreds of pages of text between us, each interaction a celebration of each other, a million mini-kindnesses layered within the domestic and philosophical chatter, I wonder if we knew that each exchange could be our last, so why not express love every time, why not tell each other how we felt?

The last text in the series was his to me. "Okay darlin." Okay, darlin, we're okay. *Sunshine, let's burn it in the sunshine.*

AUGUST 27, 2017
Begin Again

The first Saturday of February was cold, just a few degrees. We planned to go shopping for a ring. The ring had been a topic for quite a while; we had been looking at styles and scoping out ideas. Tommy couldn't wait to wear a ring, but that would wait. First, an engagement ring for me.

We decided to go to Boston. Tommy knew a few jewelers and had sketched a plan for the day. It was one of those incredibly bright, sunny days, the air thin because of the extreme cold. We stopped at Peet's to get a cup of coffee for the drive, and I suggested we try a jeweler in Wellesley, a nice store with new and estate jewelry. We looked in the window. To the right of the front door was a case with two rings. I pointed at one and said, "That's it." We laughed that imagine-if-it-were-that-easy sort of laugh and went into the store to browse.

The young saleswoman seated us and brought our choices over. I slipped on the ring we had seen in the window. It fit perfectly. Three stones from the 1920s put in a new setting, absolutely beautiful. Practical in that it wears like a band, with no stones protruding, but also one of a kind, exquisite. We went through the motions of trying on the others we had selected and learned more about the ring, but the decision was already made.

We walked out laughing, like we had pulled some kind of trick. No shopping, no searching, no agonizing, not even any refitting! Instead of going to Boston, we walked through town, past the church where we later held Tommy's memorial service, to the restaurant bar where we had our first date. Still early, "our" seats at the bar were empty. We ordered Cava and spent the afternoon eating tapas and basking in the sunshine and our good fortune.

The next time I saw the ring was on the beach in Sosua in the Dominican Republic.

We had been to this beach with the kids during a post-Christmas trip earlier that year. It was part of a resort with a spectacular restaurant with glass walls built above the rocks, the surf crashing on the glass in high seas. Small inlets were woven along the coastline, and we found ourselves a private cove. We spent the day talking and lying in the sand. Finally, in one of Tommy's cornier moments, he said, "Do you believe in hidden treasures?" He may have even included a reference to pirates. And when I looked down, the ring was there in the sand and the surf was coming up. I grabbed it! My goodness, it seemed like a crazy move. I guess the ring couldn't have been swept away by the waves, or nestled into the sand like a sand crab, but it felt that way at the time.

I cried. Does that always happen? Even if you know it's coming, even if it's what you want, even when you have talked about it? That moment was still the moment. The moment when your hopes for the future become your reality. It's scarier than you think it should be; why is there just a taste of fear, a thin thread of uncertainty to infuse life into that moment—tension, desire, fear, the full range of emotion. We went to the restaurant and had a glass of champagne. Later I had a nap. Tommy took a video of me sleeping, my shoulders registering my breath, the waves behind me.

When I look at that video now, I think that was the moment I began again. After the rigor and energy of our courtship, it was time to rest, to settle, to let the energy move through the body. In yoga, resting seems to let the movement and effort take hold in your body. After you lie in shavasana, you turn onto your right side in a fetal position, knees up to your chest, head on your arm or forehead on the floor. It is the begin-again pose. A chapter of my life had ended and a new one began.

AUGUST 29, 2017
i carry your heart (i carry it in my heart)

Within days of Tommy's death, my friend Mary Beth gave me a graphic poster of the E. E. Cummings poem "i carry your heart (i carry it in my heart)." The frame rests on my bathroom sink, so every day I am home, I see it multiple times, rereading it out loud in my mind.

But it may not have been until this trip to Rwanda, and especially the two-day trek to Uganda, that I started to understand how that might be possible. At home Tommy is everywhere; he is in every place, every room, every person, presence surrounding me. We go to Maine, and he is there; we go to Nantucket, he is there.

But then I come to East Africa, and there is a shift. He is not in the exterior world here; he is in my interior world. I see the city though his eyes; I imagine him traveling here. I think of our trip to New Zealand and how much he would love this landscape. He would love the villages; he would by now know every plant farmed, the names of every mountain or hill; he would be talking to everyone and finding out about the local building methods.

Sophie and I go to Uganda to see the gorillas, staying two nights at the beautiful Gahinga Lodge. Our little house is round with stone walls and a thatched roof, every detail perfectly crafted. While we are at dinner, someone lights our fire, and when we get into bed there are hot-water bottles warming the bed, startling Sophie.

The first night I sleep lightly. We have a 5 a.m. wakeup call to start our voyage to see the gorillas. Sophie sleeps in the van on the bumpy, two-hour-plus drive to the Bwindi Impenetrable National Park. I am awake as the sun rises at 7 a.m., so close to the equator that there is daylight from about 7 a.m. to 7 p.m. It's quiet and I soak in the spectacular landscape, observing the villages—at first dark, few people stirring, then waking up. We pass the extraordinarily still and beautiful Lake Mulehe. I feel not so much that everything I see is him, like at home, but rather that I can see through his perspective, or what I imagine it to be. It is calming to think that I know what this idea means, and that I can do it. I can carry Tommy's heart peacefully in my heart.

Sophie and I join a group of eight tourists and our guide, a woman with a machete named Peace. A guard, Eric, walks with a gun in the back. Our group is fully outfitted with hiking gear, but Sophie is wearing running shoes, and my shoes are even worse—slip-on sneakers with no treads. We're both intimidated by our lack of preparation. We start by crossing the river, with a few stones to jump between, several people falling in up to their knees. I am a little panicked. What if my feet get wet in the first ten minutes? Tommy always said that the number one survival skill in the army is to keep your feet dry. We do.

After walking along the riverbed, farmland carved into the hillside to our right and forest to our left, we cross a narrow bridge and head almost straight up for about two hours—with lots of slipping and grabbing, and some help from Eric. The gorillas are on the move, and our pace picks up. At the time, I thought Peace might be worrying that we won't find them, but in retrospect, I wonder if the drama of the chase is part of the experience. Before we know it, Eric says, "Shhh," and there is a silverback ambling toward us. We watch him, spellbound, so close, his fingers, toes, and face in vivid detail. The family starts to join him. Three mothers, another father, a three-year-old, and a six-month-old, all coming right toward us. We barely move over the next hour, transfixed by these mystical creatures. The babies are playful and climbing the trees, swinging. The adults are eating and resting. None are concerned with us.

We journey back home, filthy and tired, but happy. Our shoes were fine; we didn't need the special hiking gear after all. That night, we prepare for sleep in our cozy cottage, shutters closed, no early-morning wakeup. I note the details of the cottage to share with Tommy, I think to myself, irrationally, for future projects. How does the stone wall meet the thrush ceiling? Look at the shower detail. I go to bed not totally restful. I've lost the comforted feeling and only feel his absence at that moment.

I dream.

In my dream, I found out somehow that Tommy had five days to live. I wasn't sure the information was accurate, however. Should I tell him? What if I was wrong? That would make him unnecessarily fearful. But what if I was right? Then certainly he needed to know, so he could choose how to live those last five days. I didn't know what to do, and I couldn't get him alone to talk about it. The dream got complicated. There was panic and people were running about. There was lots of water, like a flood, but it was clean, like an aquarium tank spilling over. And there was a naked baby. I was holding her and she was slippery from the water. I knew I had to tell Tommy, but I had to hold on to the baby and he was busy rescuing people.

I woke up when I heard a knock on the door, someone with a pot of coffee for me and tea for Sophie. But I got back into bed, as if I could crawl back to that dream. For what? To resolve the ending? To know what happened? Did I tell him? Was it true? Maybe most important, what would he do with those last five days? But the fragments of the dream were lost; there were no answers.

One step forward, two steps back. I can still remember the feeling of comfort that I can carry Tommy in my heart; it feels more sweet than sad. But I also know that the overwhelming allure of his presence in my thoughts means that he is not "in" anything. I can't contain him, and I still haven't managed to relax my mind and accept his death. What if this? What if that? What if I could . . . ? What if he could . . . ? What if we'd just had a little more time to go through some of this process together, for him to guide me, give me courage, tell me what to do, let me know what he wanted. We could discuss it, as we discussed everything.

I know in my mind that I cannot rewrite reality. Tommy did not have any warning, no time; there is no bringing him back, and there is no way to recapture days or hours or even minutes. I feel the pull of my subconscious not accepting that reality, and I also know that I must, and that maybe if I do, the beauty he brought to my life can continue to unfold.

SEPTEMBER 1, 2017
Just Love

A new feeling has taken hold of me this week. Let me see if I can figure out how to describe it. I could use a word that feels negative, like "emptiness," or a word that feel more positive, like "lightness."

I'm reading a lot—books on Buddhist philosophy and reincarnation; *The Book of Joy*, a conversation between the Dalai Lama and Archbishop Desmond Tutu. I'm trying to understand how people incorporate grief into their lives and stay positive and joyous, and keep a sense of humor. That prospect felt so impossible, but I'm beginning to see it's not.

Ashes to ashes, dust to dust. What does it all mean? Is there a meaning? I thought I knew what Tommy and I were. I thought he was going to be my love and my husband for the rest of my life. My grandmother is turning one hundred next week. She was married to her first husband for thirty-five years before he died of a heart attack in his fifties. A few years later she married her second husband, and they were married for more than forty years. He was three years younger than she, and when he died a few years ago at the age ninety-three, I thought his death would change her, perhaps hasten her own death. But she continues. She still lives in her split-level house in suburban DC. Now she has full-time, live-in care, but she still climbs the stairs to her room, her main form of exercise. She has her photos, her memories, her family. She mourns my cousin. But at her big one-hundredth birthday party next week she'll be surrounded by her friends and family.

I guess I hoped that would be me. Tommy had seen his doctor for a full checkup five days before his death and was assured that he was in excellent health. When he gave up gluten, he texted me that he loved his brain gluten-free, but that "I'll be eating dark chocolate till I'm ninety, baby." There was no way to prepare for his shockingly early death. It was not ever one of the things I worried about.

And yet, I feel a bit of lightness for the first time, instead of just crushing loss. The writing is cleansing me, letting my memories caress me. The beauty, purity, and reality of our love fill me. I read through hundreds of pages of text messages, sweet nothings, back-and-forth tugs—grocery lists, departure and arrival times. But mostly love taps, consistent and constant expressions of love, and gratitude for the love we felt so palpably, again and again. Respect, admiration, excitement for each other. Listening, being a soundboard, empathy for the challenges both of us were facing. Not a single unkind word, not a single doubt, not a question mark, not a misinterpretation. Just love. It makes me feel like I do get to start over. Like I do get to begin again, here in this life, this world, this incarnation.

SEPTEMBER 7, 2017
What You Say, You Say in a Body

I wake up to three reminders. The first is from my friend Claudia. She sends me a quote from Wittgenstein: "What you say, you say in a body; you can say nothing outside this body." The second is a poem about Tommy from

Catherine, including the words "When they walked it was like dancing / When they danced it was like flying." And the energy of the day is in motion.

The third is from Tara. I arrive at class at 6 a.m. after nearly a month away and very little yoga. I have been trying to start running. Sophie and I are training together for a 10K over Thanksgiving break. Running is different. It's physical, but I don't get the runner's high. Back to work, back to school. The motions—shopping, cooking, commuting, carpooling—feel academic, removed. I have not written for a week, and now I know why: I am not in my body.

In class with Tara, there is no choice. The physical imperative sparks the mental imperative. "Stretching soft tissue releases stored tension," she says. It is there I remember that, for me, I can say nothing outside the body, think nothing outside the body.

I am in motion, only it is January 2016. Bohemia is nearly completed, and I am in New Orleans. I am in love. I wake up at the International House, alone but never alone; he is always with me. I start the day at an early yoga class on Magazine Street. Everywhere I travel—Los Angeles or Minneapolis or Seattle or Portland—I find a yoga studio, pack my yoga clothes, and go to class. The Reyn Studio, found through friends, is the embodiment of a perfect studio: second-floor loft with high ceilings, exposed beams, hand-made furniture, industrial windows, and sparkly light fixtures. The sun is rising in New Orleans, and through the black-trimmed window panes you can see the low cityscape, knowing that the river is beyond—rarely seen in everyday life here, but always present.

I am on a mission. I have a breakfast meeting with the New Orleans Redevelopment Authority and our new Rose Fellow. After breakfast, I have only a few hours before my flight. I am on foot, but I have wings. I am in motion. The first stop is the record store, a way to capture the essence of a place, bring home a few of the staff favorites. I have dreams of bringing back records from every trip, a local shopping expedition to capture this world back at home with Tommy. I choose the Meters, Irvin Mayfield, and a classic Sweet Honey in the Rock that is on sale.

We're moving into Bohemia; the space is made. The walls, ceiling, floor, windows, and bathroom are installed. The painting is finished. Now it is time for curtain rods and curtains and lights—the details that make it specific. I keep walking, determined to buy only small objects that will fit in my bag. At the antique store I collect pieces of hardware—towel hooks and coat hooks in the shape of shells and hands and antlers. The more I hunt, the more I find.

Tommy is with me, walking down the street, in my mind only of course, but just a text message away. We chitchat a bit, although I'll keep my surprises for later, bring them home and open them like presents. A brass bicycle, a coaster for his side of the bed. Brown paper cutout letters spelling B-O-H-E-M-I-A and a black piece of hardware with which to hang them. I am walking down Magazine Street and my whole self is flooded with delight: the joy in the hunt, the purchase and the surprise and the sharing, the anticipation.

So, what is the difference today in this yoga class? Would I be considered crazy if I texted him now? Can I keep that joy and that vibration of the connection alive, even if he can't respond? Now I have these artifacts and found items surrounding me, made into a place, our life. They comfort me, and yet of course they are not enough. There is a tinge of sadness; the residue of the anticipation has changed its tenor.

But I know that memory is not just a memory. It's like muscle memory; it is deep inside, the feeling of being in love and moving through space, or tingling with excitement and walking down Magazine Street, its textures and tactile sensations rising up to meet me through the cracks in the sidewalks—the roots, the pleasure of the color and the architecture, the beads and the tropical vegetation. Jungle. When I am in motion, I can almost get this feeling back.

SEPTEMBER 9, 2017

The Give and Take

"I am feeling very loinclothy today," Tommy wrote to me, packing up his apartment to move into our house. He had lived in three apartments since moving out of the family home, and lots of things were still in boxes. Plus, his stuff was scattered about. There had been a storage unit at some point. Other possessions were in Doug's basement. He had been spending so much time at our house that maybe he was also realizing what he really needed and what he didn't, so a purge was underway. Because we had been redoing the house together, I know it already felt like his, but the official move-in was still a big deal. He was culling his closet, getting rid of old clothes, making trips to the "give and take" at the recycling center. His living-room furniture ("Big Brown") finally made our finished basement that dreamy TV-watching room my house has never had.

The Sunday before he died, Mother's Day, about a year after he had moved in, he retrieved the last of his belongings from Doug's basement. Doug, his friend through this transition time, was also moving, and Tommy helped him move and took the last of his things. Most of those possessions, along with the other boxes, landed in our garage. It looks like a bomb went off in there. One corner contains his workbench in process. He was thrilled to finally have a place for his tools, and a house in which to use them. There was an elaborate reuse of tables, cabinets, tops, shelves— anything that was castaway from the house redesign found its way to the garage, and he employed all the pieces into some use. I remember thinking to myself that this was a generational thing. Is it true that people now go to the Container Store and buy things to hold things? I know my grandfather and father did not; they used the pieces and parts to make new arrangements, as Tommy did.

It seems prescient that just a few days after having assembled the last of the disparate pieces of his life under one roof (or rather house plus garage), Tommy died. "Loinclothy" is not how I would describe his possessions. There was far more than the term suggests. What is this stuff we leave behind? How does it transfer its useful life? Who cares about it? Like a dog laying a bone at its owner's feet, maybe Tommy chose to bring the stuff to me for a reason. I guess I realize now how much he trusted me. In his life, this particular thought never occurred to me, but in retrospect it does. Let me bring you all the artifacts of my life and trust you to do the right thing with them. To care enough to get them to the people who need them. To see, and sort, and read, and love. To learn more about me than I ever told you, not because I didn't want to, but just because some things don't need to be told—some histories too remote, some memories too sad, or too happy, or too personal.

But now I get to be that trusted one. To read the yearbook, to find his mother's prayer card, to sort the books that didn't make it onto the shelf or to read the application that was unsuccessful; to find the stories, photographs, videos, the life of a man that was lived long before I met him. I know the stuff is not him, but I feel honored to be the custodian. Whatever might be in those boxes, be it treasure or trash, will take time to sort, maybe by his sisters and the boys. But for now, I'll do my best to keep it dry.

SEPTEMBER 9, 2017
Welcome to the Scarab

Liv is a senior and headed to college next year. With Sophie gone already, the house feels big and empty. Tommy and I had envisioned this house full of a family of eight, knowing it would never be the boys' primary home, but optimistically making room for them. Now we are four, or three at present, and two next year.

"We should take in a boarder," Liv says, and indeed she is right. We have lots of room to share. I have already been renting it, a good way to pay for college and a chance to use the house to its advantage. Wellesley College graduation, Babson reunions. We've had people staying here from Mongolia, India, China, and all over the States. We hosted a wedding for a young couple who recently received their PhDs from MIT, prewedding weekends, and family get-togethers. It's been a wonderful way to meet new people and have them enjoy the house.

When Bates died in March 1929, she left the Scarab to Wellesley College in her will. One of the first artifacts I found was a piece of stained plywood with hooks and skeleton keys on it, with an index card dated "Dec. 8, 1952," that read "BATES WELLESLEY COLLEGE." Listed were the room rates for nightly and weekly rental:

Double Bed 2 in room $5.50 night

Double Bed 1 in room $4.00 night

Single room (Attic) $3.00 night

[Illegible] Inn—Front Room—One $4.00 night

Two $6.00 night

Weekly Rate for One person—$12.00 week

Weekly Rate for Two Persons—$18.00 week

This house, designed as a center of domestic and community life, a sort of grownup dormitory, had become too still over time. Bates's death on March 29, 1929, seems to have been peaceful, but sorrowful. She had moved up to Bohemia after Coman died in 1915; of course she did. I can only imagine what she felt at that moment, the sad comfort she would have taken at being in Bohemia, with its magical light and essence of her beloved. In *My Soul is among Lions*, Ellen Leopold recounts, "She died in 1929 in the same room as Coman, at the top of the Scarab, listening to John Greenleaf Whittier, read to her by a friend—just as she herself had recited Whittier to Coman fourteen years earlier."

She never really left, and it's a cautionary tale for me. Will I ever leave? Leopold wrote, "After publishing *Yellow Clover*, Bates turned away from the past and applied her professional energy and skills to more public concerns, such as Wellesley College and the League of Nations. Bates was shocked by the carnage of the World War I and wrote powerful poems that brought much of her private grief to bear on what she deemed a public catastrophe." Leopold does not state a cause of death. She wrote, "Katharine's quiet breathing gently ceased." It feels to me like her heart never healed; she had seemingly just lost her desire to live.

Tax records show that her housekeeper, Mrs. Mary Reddell, stayed in the house, perhaps by herself, for the rest of that year. Bates deeded the house to Wellesley College, and by 1930 it was rented to visiting faculty members. When we renovated the third floor, we found the August 22, 1931, *Saturday Evening Post* in the floorboards, featuring "Red-Headed Woman" by Katharine Bush.

Wellesley College owned the house between 1930 and 1950, during the war years, and the records show a diversity of residents. Some years showed all women. From 1943 to 1945 there were six or seven adult women living here; their professions were listed as manager, bookkeeper, dressmaker, nurse, housekeeper, at home. The men came home in 1946, and that year's tax records show eleven adults in the house (children were not recorded), including two marked as veterans. Those residents were milkman, cosmetician, dressmaker, inspector, assembler, clerk, dress fitter, engineer, and two housewives.

In 1951, Wellesley College sold the house to Harold and Vivian Jackson, who owned it for the following decade. They, too, had renters, as many as six adults at one time, including foreman, salesman, dental hygienist, insurance broker, engineer, at home. The final owners before us were Walter and Muriel Robinson, who bought the house in 1960 and lived here until their deaths. They took in renters in the 1960s, including draftsman, architect, unemployed, secretary.

The house has slept seventeen people when the Rose Fellows come for the weekend. It is a perfect place for these large gatherings, and I know it's the dream that Bates and Coman had for the space. It exudes a warm welcome, and I think of Bates's friends and family who remembered her standing stoutly on the front steps, calling out "Welcome to the Scarab!" to her guests.

SEPTEMBER 10, 2017

The Gap: The Boundless Map

> For what happens at the moment of death is that the ordinary mind and its delusions die, and in that gap the boundless skyline nature of our mind is uncovered.
> —Sogyal Rinpoche

What is death? I realize I have so little idea. I was completely unprepared for this moment. Did I miss the memo? Or is this a lesson delivered only to those who must learn it in the moment? I am reading up, splitting my time between stories of grief (*The Light of the World*; *Option B*), and books on living and dying (*The Tibetan Book of Living and Dying; Many Lives, Many Masters*). I know there is no sure answer, but I want to at least know what is known.

I am surprised to learn that Brownie Wheeler, a neighbor from Taconnet, our island community in Maine, wrote a book called *One Life, Many Deaths: A Surgeon's Story*. This brings an incredibly abstract concept intimately close to home. He describes near-death experiences and stories of his patients going "to the other side" and returning. I knew Brownie as a seemingly ancient and very tall man, a tennis player and lake lover. I never would have imagined that he was the author of a book like this, with his Harvard degree and Boston practice.

In those brief moments of his death, what did Tommy experience? Was it a feeling of cessation of pain, of ease and no worry, of light and going toward it? Is there such a thing as heaven, and is he reunited with Andy, his parents, and other friends? Does he get to hang out with Ernie Davis and Muhammed Ali?

Was he watching us that morning? Did he see that moment I left his side? As usual after yoga class, my clothes were soaking wet, as if I had jumped into the lake. I was with him the whole time except for that one moment when I went to put on dry clothes. I thought it would be a long day. I knew we were going to the hospital, but I assumed we would be there for a while. How long did it take me? Ten seconds? Fifteen? Not long. I was wearing sweatpants and a hoodie. When I talked to my mom on the phone, I asked her to bring me a bra.

Why these prosaic details? Why focus on the moments of human reality in the midst of this existential event? Yet I wonder what he experienced. Did he float above us? I can almost relive that morning from the ceiling of the yoga studio, looking down like it's a floor plan. I see the man at the center, the women on the edges, the woman at the center coming and going with gravitational pull and the need to release. I see Caroline and the fear in her eyes, unsure of where her body should be in space. I see myself, the woman at the center, knowing where to be, right with him, but then this moment of thinking ahead—the ambulance, the hospital, making calls, calling the cardiologist, planning the best treatment option, the best hospital, calling my mom, the girls, school, where are they, my phone, it's at home, my clothes drenched through. I need to change. Is that really what I need to do? Yes, actually it is. I am drenched, and the EMTs are there, and it will take only a second, but still.

My view expands and I see the larger frame, not just the studio and those of us in it, but now Tara running. She's gone to get my phone. On foot. She doesn't know where I live, but she takes off, running. I can follow her path in my mind's eye. She calls Liv, who is at school, so early, and the view I have expands to include the high school and Liv in the lunchroom. I see Tommy still at the center, the EMTs working, Tara running, Liv answering the phone, bursting into tears. What was Tommy seeing in those moments? If he died in that moment, how long did that moment last, that infinite instant? And if he indeed allowed his body to remain still there on the floor, but his soul or his spirit (what is the right name for this?) to elevate, could he see this map of his world in motion? If so, how long did that last and how far did it go? My map expands to include the calls from the ambulance to Tommy's sons—one already heading west on Route 9 at that early hour, one close by in Brookline, one on the Cape. All the way to Sophie in Denver, a sort of "find my friends" map of my world, everyone mobilizing, gravitating to the center, to Tommy, to me, to be together. Did he see the boys racing to the hospital, did he hear them, feel them with him? Was he still in the hospital room as Bliss sat by his side and told him, for no less than an hour, everything he meant to her?

Can he see us still? Could it be true that he is now with me in the ultimate form of the journey we started together? Can he see into my heart and the dark crevices of my mind? Can he see my base humanity, and the need to change clothes, for God's sake? I'd love to think so. I love the thought that he can, in fact, now see everything in my heart and mind. Such a relief, after all, to have the last of the barriers taken down, to finally ditch the facade of language and pierce directly to my core.

I don't know, but I bet he has other things to do than watch our every move. I think that at some essential level he trusts us. He forgives me for taking those seconds to change my clothes; he would not have wanted me to be soaking wet in the ambulance and at the hospital. He knows my inner darkness the same way he knows my inner light; it's the same to him, it's just me. He has his own lessons to learn and lives to lead. He will never leave us, but he will trust us.

Unless, of course, he is simply gone. As gone as he is on earth, could he possibly be that gone in the universe? My yoga teacher, Jordan, would say no, energy never dies or is created; it is only recycled. But in so many heartbreaking ways, he is gone. He is not at Bliss's first diving meet tonight. But there she is, somehow, fearlessly diving. Maybe he is there, giving her that courage. He is not in bed, on the train, at the station; he is not on the porch or in the kitchen or coming home late. He is so very clearly not here. And yet, whatever the parameters of faith or belief or fantasy, I know that he has changed me forever. "I am not going back," Sue Ann reminds me that I said, right from the beginning. I am not going back to the person I was, or was perceived to be, before I met him.

I am now getting the memo that he is gone. I am even starting to accept it. I won't begin to accept the wisdom of this—surely there is none—but I am beginning to accept the reality. The glimmer of hope—the reason to get up, to read and write, and to smile—is that his life on earth has traction, momentum. It has lessons that are not just learned but actualized; it has meaning that transcends his physicality. I feel his love for me and for us. I feel his stillness at the center, as we all spin and draw close to him at the hour of his death. I feel his love as I sob and mourn and run and read. I am learning these lessons about dying and living with him, in perhaps a way that is more profound than if he were here reading beside me in bed.

SEPTEMBER 13, 2017
Muscle Memory

My neighbor across the street, ever vigilant of the activities in our house, tells the story of watching us come home from yoga, day after day, at around 7 a.m., and clasping hands for the walk from the car to the house. It's a busy time of day, with kids to be woken, breakfast, showers, drive to school, walk to train. Why join hands for those 15 feet?

I can live a whole lifetime in those ten or twelve strides from the car to the front door. We would hold hands, even for that short distance. From train to platform, from house to car, from yoga studio and up the stairs. I remember the first time Tommy and I held hands; it felt like a revelation. He told me later that in that moment the pieces fell into place for him. There was some sort of recognition of the rightness and necessity of us, as if linking hands linked our lives in some essential way. I can still feel the palm of his hand on the palm of my hand. The muscle memory of my right arm reaching out. It seems that it was most often my right hand; that is the hand I feel him with, fingers intertwined.

The fact that it felt so natural doesn't mean it was unconscious. Form follows function, function follows form. I watch my sister's parents-in-law, now in their early eighties, walk through town holding hands. They seem a unit, so fluid and connected, and I notice they are always holding hands— at the game, in the rink, on the street.

"Time expands for us" maybe applies to this moment as well. Could it be that we lived a whole life in that short distance? It feels that way, as though space expanded and time slowed as long as we were holding hands, that the present moment could last a lifetime.

SEPTEMBER 15, 2017
Buried Treasure

Found in garage: this treasure, a leather briefcase with brass hinges and buckles. Inside, the loot. Three navy-blue cases with gold-embossed patterning and writing (United States of America), containing six ROTC medals and some lapel pins. Also in the briefcase:

- Commander's Handbook for Property Accountability at Unit level (September 1980)
- How to Succeed in the Army National Guard, by really trying
- A Study of Organizational Leadership from 1976
- Code of Conduct for Members of the Armed Forces, 1978
- Orders from the Rhode Island Army National Guard to report on

Active Duty to Vicenza, Italy, on August 29, 1988, with the Purpose: DISPLAY DETERMINATION
- Pins, lapel notes from an award speech (family support! BIGGEST ACCOMPLISHMENT!) [his emphasis]
- Ticket stub from Monday, December 6, 2010, Patriots / Jets game (Section 119, Row 1, Seat 15)
- 2007 Red Sox World Series Watch

The home-run find is Tommy's application to Harvard Business School dated March 4, 1991. He had told me about applying and being turned down. He writes clearly about his father's death, high school, and getting to college. He tells a side of the story that I hadn't heard, that while he ended up with a full scholarship to URI, this was no guarantee in his first year. I am reminded of his high school friend telling me that in the college application process, there was no one looking out for Tommy. He took out a loan that first semester, but it would be his last. He earned his spot on the football team and got a full scholarship, making captain and getting the fifth-year award and the student athlete award.

In the essay, he talks about the dilemmas he faced in the 1043d Combat Support Company, one of the largest National Guard units in the Northeast: "I remain deeply touched by the confidence and pride displayed by the members of the 1043d Combat Support Company, and the opportunity to serve as their commander is something I will always treasure." He talks about his deployment to participate in a large NATO exercise in Italy and Turkey.

I think of Liv now working on her college applications, how hard it is to be clear about who you are, and about how what you have done influences who you are and who you hope to become. It's hard to be clear about your strengths while not feeling like you are bragging.

"Early in my military career, I discovered that the most significant barrier preventing me from realizing my leadership potential was a tendency not to take full account of the ideas and reactions of associates and subordinates," he wrote. "A somewhat self-righteous personal attitude based on legitimate power was of limited effectiveness and was detrimental to overall mission. By not tempering self-confidence, I was less receptive to the ideas and constructive criticism of others. I learned that the key to success in leadership lies in the ability to influence and a willingness to act rather than forcing compliance. I continuously strive to improve this ability to recognize the clues and the inferences of others, to accept criticism and to be a great listener. Indeed, these are the traits which I regard highly in others."

I am not sure who got into the Harvard Business School class of 1994, but I have a hard time believing they were a better investment than Tommy. He didn't get in, and it bugged him. But I love to read how he worked at listening, at kindness, at these leadership and empathy skills he became so famous for in his life. I love to think that, Harvard or not, he set himself on a life journey that he fulfilled. The military language reflects where he was in his life at that time, but the core essence of this quality of leadership would be his forever.

SEPTEMBER 17, 2017

Tears

What is the word for that boy from high school who leaves an indelible mark on you? I am leaving for college, and we have had the best summer together, a sweet moment in time. "Don't cry," he tells me. "Just don't cry." That's the way it's going to be. The rules of adolescent dysfunction agreed upon, I stop crying.

But we grow up, it turns out. After that first decade of turbulence, this friend and I chose a new pattern. And at some point, we made an agreement to be kind to each other above all else. In my kitchen is a print he made that says, "NOTE TO SELF: BE KIND, BE KIND; BE KIND," an atonement of sorts for those emotionally fraught years.

We talk on the phone after Tommy's death. I can hear in his voice that he wants to hear it all from me. I am grateful for the chance because I am still processing the events; there are some things I'm grasping to understand. At the would-be wedding day, Tara told the group of friends and family that Tommy was not scared. I loved hearing her say that, but I don't think it's true. I think he was in pain, physical and emotional, if that's the right word. His body was clearly in pain as he described the feelings: "My arms are numb"; "I can't feel my tongue." He didn't panic, but that doesn't mean he wasn't scared lying there on the floor, surrounded by the EMTs, losing feeling in his body, aware of the loss, tracking it.

He had perfected the practice of reading the clues and inferences of others and letting them lead in their way. I think he knew at some level, that day, because of everything that happened that morning: the fact that he stayed with me instead of going to Providence, the weather and the beautiful pink sunrise, the lovemaking, the bliss of the coffee, the fully articulated words of love, the perfection of the class and being able to practice next to each other, his hand on my back. I know that he did not know consciously, but I feel that somewhere inside himself, he knew and he had to make sure to let me know: "Babe, I am getting ready to go, and I want you know that everything I have had with you was so perfect, and I love you so much."

I describe this scene to my friend as I've been exploring it in my mind over these months. Touching Tommy, I can feel his pain, but holding his hand helps; I know it. I am like a morphine drip to him; my touch eases the pain, but it doesn't make the fear go away. "Katie!" he cries. "I'm right here with you, baby." He is leaving. He wants to stay, but he can't; he is leaving his body, and it hurts.

At the other end of the phone line I hear sobbing. Sobbing? I am telling my story, deep in exploration, still inquiring; I am working hard. And I am crying, but lo and behold, he is crying too. Loudly. Thirty years later, this high school boyfriend and I cry together. Not over us, or a version of our teenage selves. We cry together over life and love and loss. We cry for Tommy and for me and for him too maybe, and I know perhaps for the first time since I was thirteen and he was fourteen that this boy / man loves me.

These tears that flow, what are they? There may have been a time in our lives when people were able to make us cry, as in "I didn't mean to make you cry." But those days seem distant now. There is no one and nothing that can make me cry that way anymore, at least I hope not. But tears themselves—the embodiment of sadness and struggle and life and death—are perhaps meant to be shared. It may take us a very long time in a relationship, thirty years even, to evolve to the place where we can cry together, but it feels like a step in the right direction. We don't force ourselves on each other; we just bear witness. We commiserate—for our own reasons, no doubt, but the tears come from the same place.

SEPTEMBER 18, 2017
The Rest Is Silence

When the alarm goes off this morning, I am momentarily lost, woken from deep sleep. It's pitch-black in Bohemia. The room has seventeen windows, so the blackness means there is no starlight. It's only September and still warm out, but already winter's darkness is coming.

I have gotten my paperwork in order. My will, a trust set up for the girls, my healthcare proxy. I have more to do, but I am determined not to procrastinate. Clear-eyed now that I will die, it's just a matter of when; I want to be ready for those left behind. But I realize this morning what I am missing. The healthcare proxy is incomplete. No, don't keep me on life support; yes, I want to be cremated; yes, I am a full organ donor. But what else would I add now?

I want to die in May or on a summer day. If I die in winter, it had better be in some temperate climate. I want to die on a beautiful day. I want to have told someone that I love them that day. I want to be doing something I love. I want someone whom I love to hold my hand. I want to feel in harmony with my life, loved ones, and the universe.

Despite the dark, I get up and go to yoga. I have learned that lesson fully by now—just get there and the rest will take care of itself. I feel good today. I'm moving freely and Tara is in fine form; the class is full and there are lots of new people in the room, the get-back-to-school energy pushing them. I notice that a few people who started last fall are still coming; now it's their habit too, and I am happy for them.

My high school's motto, "Sound Mind in Sound Body," has been in my head. I have been exercising my body more, and it feels good to get back into my yoga routine and to add running. I was sore last week for the first time in a while. Sound mind, yes, I am trying. I have been reading everything I can get my hands on, working to intellectually understand death and dying, love and living.

But I know now that while both sound mind and sound body are important, the motto is missing an essential component: sound spirit. It is becoming obvious that this is where it all needs to happen. Running a marathon or reading a book won't get you to the place of peace; it's as clear to me as the morning sky was pink on May 17.

In class, Tara plays "Imagine" and I am lifted back to our rental car in New Zealand. I am driving and we are singing. Tommy is navigating, narrating, and teaching me to sing. The song is "Imagine." I have to learn the lyrics better to sing without the song playing in the background, and he is walking me through it. "And the world will be as one." He told me time and time again that we were one. It was like a mantra: our one plus one made one; the idea of oneness was a guiding force.

Cruising through that dramatically beautiful countryside inside our bubble, it was not hard to imagine living for today—no possessions, no country, no greed, no hunger. We were traversing the sky and mountains, hills and oceans; they felt like heaven on earth, and the world and its people were sharing and kind.

Back at home, even in the hustle and bustle of ordinary life, it's easy for me to touch this otherworldliness. My spirit is somehow freed from my mind and my body, and I can touch this place; I can feel the vibration of his memory. "The Rest Is Silence" is the name of a sonnet Katherine Lee Bates wrote after her mother's death—a beautiful, heartbreaking phrase. I feel the infinite meanings within these few simple words. The poet, again, rescuing me.

5

Do Saints Go Gypsying in Paradise?

SEPTEMBER 20, 2017
Bohemian Ukulele

The procedure was easy. I had finally gone in last week to check out a spot on my forehead. It had been there for months, but I did my best to ignore it over the summer. It was a basal-cell carcinoma, and today the doctor took it out. It is my second, so extra vigilance is required, but it is manageable. What I hadn't fully anticipated, however, was the experience of being there on the table. Certainly, a calmer environment than the emergency room, but still a place that brought memories flooding back.

Am I getting better? I think so, at least some of the time. Life has gone back to normal, or rather the "new normal," as Sophie says, and, by the way, nothing about it is "back." School, sports, work, dinnertime, lunches, carpool, college applications, all the stuff of life. And while no one has forgotten, the world moves on. I can't decide where that puts me. Am I supposed to be moved on too? Am I "stuck" in my grief? Or am I simply grieving?

It's been four months, but some of it I remember like it was yesterday—the minutes in the studio, the ambulance ride, the minutes at the hospital "before" and the hours "after"—like a slow-motion movie in my mind. I am now more capable of turning those images off, but they are there, at the ready, when I allow them. Today the flashback takes me by surprise—something about the smell, the glare of lights, the doctors and nurses.

There is a pause in the action. They will run a test under the microscope and I will wait, eyes closed, on the bed. I am tired and think I might sleep. The doctors and nurses are chatting at the station right outside my room. It took me back to what had been the worst night of my life on May 22, 2008, the night after my mitral-valve repair. A five-hour, open-heart procedure followed by a night in intensive care, two nights at the hospital. The old Brigham and Women's Hospital was designed with a nurses' station in the middle of a circle of rooms. All through that first night I could hear the idle chatter of the nursing team. They talked—about their kids, their divorces; I heard so much of this conversation I could have repeated it the next day. The hospital was designed as if the patient's experience was irrelevant. The nurses spoke freely, as if the patients were not even there. Which I, for one, was and wasn't, still heavily sedated. I will never forget them making me stand up the first time after the surgery, feeling the rush of anesthesia coursing through me, a nausea and sick feeling worse that I have ever felt physically, the toxicity of it.

All in the name of a cure, and I had one, so who cares? At the time of my heart surgery, I remember being grateful that it was my heart. Boston is renowned for its medical community and certainly its cardiac care. My surgeon was one of the early inventors of the "mini" mitral-valve repair and had perfected it over the hundreds of times he had performed this surgery. I was in good hands; I was not to worry.

When it seemed that Tommy was having a heart attack, I thought, good, we can deal with that. I called my mother from the yoga studio. We are going to the hospital. Tommy may have had a heart attack. Call Dr. Adler and tell him we are coming. I have an excellent cardiologist; he is connected to the best in Boston; this is just something we need to handle, I thought.

Meanwhile in the yoga studio, the four EMTs, the cop, Tara, Caroline, and I are buzzing around Tommy. He is getting quiet, but surely he can hear. The idle chatter, the underlying tension, calling my mom, asking her to bring me a bra, the IV going in, poorly the first time. What does he hear? We are not going to the Brigham, they tell me; we are going to Framingham Union. Too far, too much traffic, they say. Too dead, I realize now, no time left. Perhaps by the time we reach the emergency room, he cannot hear. Is "he" still there, can "he" still hear? I keep talking to him; maybe my voice will drown out the other voices. I keep touching him, his feet mostly; perhaps my touch is warmer and more real than the crispy sheets and the hands pumping on his chest.

We are not at Framingham Union, or the Brigham. I am just an outpatient at the dermatologist's office in Chestnut Hill. The sheets are still crisp and the doctors and nurses are as nice as they can be. "A little Bohemian ukulele for you," the doctor says as he walks in with the news that my margins are clear, easy as pie. Bohemian ukulele? Who would have thought the doctor would be playing that particular music? This is definitely not the emergency room. I am fine, I am safe. When it is my turn to die, someone will be there, holding my feet.

They know I am grieving since the tears have been coursing down my cheeks. To be fair, it's sort of a lot to process. Where is my person? My person to call when I get the news, good or bad? My person to call when I am done? What happens if . . . ? Horribly morbid thoughts. I know that if Tommy were here, this doctor visit would be a nonevent, just something to handle. Frankly, something easy to handle.

I tell them about Bohemia, and the teaching assistant doctor asks me if I have read *The Year of Magical Thinking*. We talk about her undergrad literature degree and the professors and books that changed her life. One undergrad professor gave her a signed copy of an Atul Gawande book after she completed her medical degree, and they have stayed in touch. The staff are lovely; they have healed me. They love literature and the music is playing. I may not be moving on, but I am moving forward. I get up, get dressed, and drive myself home.

SEPTEMBER 22, 2017
And I'll Fly on the Wings of a Butterfly

The first thing I did when the girls and I moved into this house in summer 2007 was to tear out the dropped ceiling on the third floor. There was a lot of work to do everywhere, but this would be the most satisfying place to start. In that act, my feelings about the house changed radically. I could understand later why someone installed these panels at about 7 feet. The roof had no insulation, so the upper floor was cold in the winter and hot in the summer, and the temperature was difficult to moderate. But still, the travesty!

Under the dropped ceiling was a vaulted ceiling with tongue-and-groove panels hugging the roofline. The wood on the walls and ceiling had been stained and perhaps aged over time; they were such a dark brown they were almost black. The room, I would later learn, resembled a ship with its curved lines and beautiful wood. For now, we would just paint it and let it be. But I could see that the paneled roofline was continuous, even though the bathroom, closets, and hall still had a dropped ceiling.

The space now is a revelation. Being up here teaches me so much. I have learned what architecture means, simply that the experience of a space changes the way you think about the world. It's truly an experiential wonderland. So many factors contribute—the shape and texture of the ceiling and walls; the scarab form revealed in the roofline, with two points and outstretched wings; the tree house effect of being up in the air, watching the snow fall outside the window; the winter sky; sunrise and sunset visible for miles. In summer I'm living in the trees, which turn a vibrant yellow in the fall, flooding the room with color.

Thinking about the process that resulted in this space may be the thing I love the most, because it feels like Tommy and I were at our most fluid here. He had a way of being with me that allowed me to be my best, the self that was most realistic and optimistic. He had learned over time that my first response would not be my last. I learned that I have a habit of responding immediately to things, and often voicing that response or acting on it. But then I take some time to walk around the issue, often coming to a different conclusion. This process often happens in yoga class. Tommy was the master of the pause. He could let the first response sit there, not necessarily reacting to it, just letting it be. He trusted that I would find the right answer over time.

I had drawn plans for the third floor before we started demolition. They followed the existing plan of the large room spanning the east side of the house in a north-to-south direction. That was how we had always experienced the space, so it made the most sense at the time. But as we started taking down the walls and dropped ceiling, the way I saw the space changed. The ceiling's shape and volume became so present, and a new understanding of the complicated roofline in the front, the light, and the views took shape. We paused.

It took a month to redraw the plans and resubmit them to the building department. There was no real drama in this, just a pause in the activity to rethink and get it right. Rather than orienting the main space north–south, our new plan divided the space in the other direction, with the bathroom and closet on the north side, and the entire east-south-west space facing the backyard in an open plan. This move enhanced the room's original feeling of being a screened porch in the sky. Dorothy Burgess recounts, "With the coming of autumn, Miss Coman returned to 'Bohemia,' the wide room in the Scarab where the windows looked out to the treetops and the sky."

We would go upstairs every morning and every night after work to see and feel the space as it emerged, considering our plans. Tommy held me to my loftiest goals while I worried about taking down and replacing the paneling. Such a waste.

"You've always wanted to have this house fully insulated. We will do it," he said. We took the entire ceiling and walls back to the studs, recycling the tongue-and-groove wood, and later insulating the space with high-quality spray foam insulation so that I don't need to need to use the room heater in the winter; the one register from the house is enough to warm the space. Fernando's talented carpenters finished the complex roofline with new board and batten that hugs its dramatic shape.

From January to May we lived in and outfitted Bohemia, enjoying it fully. I will cherish those days as much as any in my life. It was like a dream come true, living here together. I could feel something shift in both of us, and he spoke about it too. He was so glad to be truly at home. Bliss loved to come up and find him here after school. Some days he would get home from site visits and meetings and take a twenty-minute nap on the couch, spread out, facing east, feet on the arm, and relax before returning to his email and work at the end of the day. Bliss would also sleep on the couch sometimes, wanting to be up here with us in our cocoon.

And now? I feel like the space is still holding me. It's an animate part of my life, as though a whole world unfolds up here, perhaps a world within a world. It is absolutely full of him; it is him in some ways, but it's a comfortable and uplifting place for me too. More than a year into her cancer but still traveling abroad, Coman wrote to Bates as she returned home: "I shall be glad to be at home and at work once more. My desk in Bohemia seems a pleasant prospect and it is good to have a congenial task ahead of me."

This ceiling line alone, like the wings of a butterfly. Oh, baby, "I'll go wherever you go. I am along for this journey with you, without you; wherever you take me I'll go."

SEPTEMBER 28, 2017
Commuter

The closet is full of shoes: walking shoes, commuting shoes, boots. Like a kid in a candy store, I bought him shoes. Size 11, built for walking, riding, sprinting to the train. When I first met him, he was chained to his car. He drove me to work, to my home, to the airport. Who cared about the traffic when there was so much to talk about, so much music to play, and so many stories to tell? It was an act of love, but then there was an infinitely better way to be together.

First I got him a train app and a pair of Ecco sneakers—smart-looking gray leather with a white sole, sharp enough to wear to work. A pair of Blundstones, a must-have shoe for the stylish and practical winter commuter and hockey dad, with thick warm socks inside. Commuting meant leaving the house on foot and figuring out the rest of his sometimes complicated days on the fly. Essential gear consisted of headphones, backpack, battery charger, sunglasses. If you get wet, he delighted, you just dry off. Prisoner of the car no more!

In the Bates/Coman days, the train operated more like a streetcar. You can hear the train from the house, especially from Bohemia on the south side. The 5:35 a.m. train is always the signal that it's time to leave for yoga. You can also hear the trains pulling into the station in Wellesley Square from Boston, and as Tommy walked up to the house from the train station, about a half mile away, Bliss would call from the kitchen window, "Tommy NI-LES!" And a happier man never existed. As we left the house on foot together, walking quickly to catch the train, never a minute to spare, a happier woman never existed. Alone on the train, I had perfected the coffee nap. I got up around 5:10 a.m. for yoga and by 8 a.m. would be ready for a catnap on the train. A trick: drink a nice, hot cup of coffee while waiting for the train, board for the twenty-two-minute ride to Boston, close eyes for twenty minutes. Arriving at Back Bay, I'd have had a rest and then the caffeine would hit my bloodstream—go! When I rode with him, I might rest my head on his shoulder, but mostly we held hands, lives folding into each other's. We planned most of the details of Bohemia on the train, making lists and sketching in his graph paper Moleskine as we rode. Coming home, he'd get on at South Station; I'd meet him at the next station in our spot in the last car.

The train is still there, just a hunk of metal, often late. A kind conductor here, a rude one there, a million handheld devices rendering all human interaction null and void. The walk is still nice—Dartmouth, Clarendon, Berkeley, Arlington. Good streets, a good city, alphabetically mapping the walk, no chance of getting lost. But lost still, lost in purpose, lost in tears, lost in sadness, lost in loss.

What will happen to these shoes, his beautiful boots? Does anybody want them? Goodness knows that if they fit me, I would wear the soles thin. No one has asked for them yet, shockingly. Maybe Goodwill will find them an energetic walker, one who wants to feel the Tommy Niles joy of life, the energy that pulsed within him as he navigated the world like a child with a new bike.

OCTOBER 4, 2017
Big Brown

It's fair to say that Tommy's absence still feels surreal. A guest is in town, and we watch a movie in the basement on Big Brown. I realize I have not sat down there since May, barely leaving Bohemia. When Tommy moved in, his couch and TV were brought to our basement, making our house finally one of those cool houses with a great space to watch TV. There's no couch like Big Brown, wide-wale corduroy with just the right depth and coziness. Perhaps the single best couch in the world. I first encountered this couch in Tommy's apartment in Needham—stolen moments alone in his bachelor pad. Then the couch moved to his apartment in Wellesley; it made a home wherever it landed. When it came to the basement of the Scarab, we had to take the door off the hinges, remove the door frame and trim, and rebuild the wall after it was in. It wasn't meant to move again. It was supposed to have found its ultimate home, one way or the other. I guess it has.

But where is Tommy? I can practically feel his body next to me, the length of him, the feel of him. I can hear his words, watch him getting up and down, making sure all is set; everyone has everything they need, ready to settle in, ready to spring into action at any moment. My mind's eye hardly has to work to retrieve these images, it's so visceral. I mean, honestly, it's crazy, right? Is it true that this glorious man, this vibrant being, is just somehow gone, seemingly evaporated into thin air? I know he was here, I know it. I know that wasn't a dream. I mean, I never could have dreamed up a couch as comfortable as Big Brown, and I barely know how to turn on a TV. How can this be, how can this be, how can this be?

It's undeniably true, and yet it's impossible. The texture of the corduroy on my palm is familiar, soothing, yet missing the warmth of your palm.

OCTOBER 8, 2017
Get Home

I flirt with the bartender.

It wasn't planned; in fact, the opposite. I'd driven to watch Bliss's afternoon diving meet in Canton and then took her to her hockey game in Milton, dropping her at the rink at around 7 p.m. for an 8 p.m. game. I needed to get gas, and then, since I had time, decided to get a bite to eat. Google took me to the slightly run-down but quaint Main Street of Hyde Park. I'd been there once before, I realized, but during the day for work, wondering if that affordable-housing project near the train station ever got built.

There was a decent-looking restaurant with a bar and live music, fairly empty on this Thursday night, one threesome at the bar and a few tables full. I sat at the bar and ordered a Caesar salad and glass of red wine. The bartender was cute, with dark hair and an easy smile, youngish, and I didn't think anything of smiling and chatting a bit. This place was owned by his friend; he filled in sometimes. It used to be a favorite hangout for Mayor Menino and had that Boston neighborhood vibe. But as we chatted, I felt his energy level rising. "He's flirting with me," it dawned on me, like a surprise. Flirting felt like something from a distant planet.

But it seemed easier to laugh and smile than let the tears well up and overflow, as they so often do. I have only thirty minutes, maybe less, I thought to myself. Could I sit here for thirty minutes and laugh and smile and make small talk? No tears. No tragic story.

A few days later, I had breakfast with a former colleague whose fiancé had died of cancer the year before. Thirty-two years old, he was her primary caretaker over the grueling eight months from diagnosis to death. We spoke about his experience handling his grief, their love story, the new foundation he helped launch in her name. He has just moved to Boston for graduate school, a new chapter. He tries to choose, now, to whom he tells what. Maybe he doesn't have to share his story with the guy sitting next to him in class. Dating again, he's learned not to bring it up on the first date. Sometimes his tattoo gives it away. "Get home" is written in her handwriting on his right forearm, high enough to not be seen with shirt sleeves, but he's a roll-up-your-sleeves kind of guy. Her last text to him: Get Home.

Maybe I'll get a tattoo, I think, imagining variations on T.E.N. or X, or TEN/10 engraved on my body. Or maybe I could write "Okay, darlin,'" although it occurs to me that I might never be able to stop the tears from spilling over when I see it.

At the bar with the cute bartender, I kept my left hand with my engagement ring in my lap. Not hiding it exactly, but who am I kidding? Pretending a bit is part of flirting, isn't it? I guess my ring is my tattoo for now. How long will I wear it? Switch from left hand to right? I can't seem to take it off, but I don't know the rules on this one. Engagement is a declaration of love and a promise of a future. Can this ring be the one without the other? It's the most beautiful piece of jewelry I can ever imagine having. How could I possibly take it off?

I don't have to make any decisions now. I feel sort of proud of my thirty-minute flirting session. Happy to hear about music and Nashville, a career shift, a daughter; happy to feel chemistry and energy flowing; happy to have a handsome man circle me, moving gracefully around the bar and out to the kitchen and dining room, to bring me dinner and fill my glass while I sit calmly still, smiling, eyes shining but no tears, hands in lap.

OCTOBER 10, 2017
TEN/10

1010 Hoffman in Elmira loomed large in the Tommy Niles stories. I've written already about the day Robbie Brewer's dad came to buy the house and how Tommy and Robbie ending up becoming friends, playing basketball in the driveway. They remained friends until Tommy's death, and Robbie and his wife, Karen, have stayed close to me. That house was magical for Tommy, and I'm beginning to understand this better now.

On the day of the would-be wedding, Harry set up his video camera to capture stories from Tommy's dearest friends with the idea to eventually make a video for his grandkids. His sisters, Mary Jane and Connie, spoke together to the camera, telling stories of growing up, the life and energy in the house before their dad died, the games, plays, songs. Their dad was strict and the kids were well behaved, but they knew how to have fun. They would set up a "houseboat" in the living room on Friday nights. Thrilled that their dad would allow them to keep it up overnight (it had to be put away by noon on Saturday), they created this wonderful, imaginative play space. Tommy, the youngest, was the builder of the crew.

The sisters described the plays and singing. Margi, his oldest sister, used to plan an elaborate Christmas pageant, and Tommy would play the angel. The girls dressed him in a white silk slip; with his rosy cheeks and a halo, he was perfect for the role. Until, that is, their father clamped down—no more slips on his son. The sisters also recounted a car trip to a family wedding where they sang "Jesus Christ Super Star" in four-part harmony. Later, in their adult lives, his sisters would sing to Tommy on the phone. The beloved baby brother, a house full of song. They knew every word of "Think about Your Troubles" by Harry Nilsson (*The Point!*) and sang beautifully, their harmonies playing off one another.

I love thinking about this side of Tommy. Things got rough after their dad died and their mom was on her own. The older siblings gradually left home, and then it was just Tommy and his mom, taking care of each other.

Mary Jane told another story that she knew her proud mother would not want told. One afternoon when Mary Jane and Tommy were home alone and he was twelve or thirteen, she opened the bread box and out came a mouse, scurrying over her hand. She screamed for Tommy, who came and "took care of it." It sounds so achingly similar to our house, to our mice, to us calling "Tommy!" It's also achingly similar to the happiness we felt with him in our household: delight in each other's presence, the fun, music, and games.

His father called him Ten, which spelled out his initials, Thomas Edward Niles, of 1010 Hoffman—a lifelong perfect TEN in our books. #TEN/10.

OCTOBER 13, 2017
Buried Treasure

The garage is nearly in order. During his move-in, Tommy made many attempts at organizing the garage, some things going to the recycling center while more things kept arriving. By last May it was overflowing, and it had gotten worse over the summer. I want to retrieve the boys' hockey bag before the season begins, but then I realize so much of their lives is there: handmade cards for their parents, report cards—those must be saved, but also sports equipment, a mildewed bag of clothes, and random items that need to be sorted and packed. So, I start there. A friend, Wendy, helps, and we get all the boys' belongings into a neat pile, fill a small pickup, and make the delivery.

Another Saturday workday is scheduled; Wendy will come back, along with some high school boys to make runs to the give-and-take. And I am so happy that Andrew Colucci is coming. He arrives bearing gifts, as it seems he always does. These gifts are extravagant in their love and thoughtfulness. He brings a bench, an absolutely stunning bench designed and handcrafted by one of the Colucci brothers. It fits in my front hall like it was designed for it, and its sculptural richness elevates the experience of coming home. Another Colucci gift arrives via email that afternoon from another brother, this one a musician, who sends an original song in Tommy's honor, remembering the great Tommy Niles, age seventeen, stopping to say to ten-year-old Dave, "You gotta good ear, kid; keep playing."

Andrew happily joins us on the garage project. Everything comes out onto the driveway. This had been a sort of ritual for Tommy, but then he'd put it all back. To be fair, he would have used that scrap wood someday, and I know I never will. And half the stuff was mine from before we met, so he didn't get rid of that. And then it was too much of a mess to get clarity. But with Wendy's gift for organizing and Andrew's gift for memory, we make progress. Most of my old stuff goes, one hopes to be used by someone else. Tommy's stuff gets organized and repacked.

He started making himself a tool bench, the old-fashioned kind, with pieces of leftover furniture: kitchen cupboards, tables, sets of drawers— random pieces put to use. The tools and hardware are an enormous mess. I think about his father, who built the garage at 1010 Hoffman and kept a productive workbench. We put anything related to the tools in one big pile. We saved the hand tools and matched up the power tools with their cords and batteries. We pitched the miscellaneous things like used roller covers and took the paint to the dump. The most precious item, a hammer Bliss had given him for Christmas, inscribed with "Tommy, excited to build memories with you. Love, Blissie;" that, we leave where he had hung it, but turn it around, the inscription facing in.

What was I looking for? I found his mother's prayer card, every album from high school, every report card since kindergarten, every newspaper article his mother must have clipped in high school. I found the awards for buildings—small plaques he put on the wall. I have sorted most of his earthly possessions by now.

I loved every discovery but also yearned constantly for more. Could I find another card? Another writing? Can we find another song he recorded, another piece of the puzzle that was him? These pieces and parts will surely keep coming—a call from an old friend, a deepened understanding, more stories, more conversation. The physical leave-behinds tell a part of the story, but ultimately, they, too, tell only so much. Having Andrew with me on this journey is the best part. We talk and talk, covering forty-five years of stories, ideas, thoughts, and feelings; we laugh. And I feel remarkably well when he leaves. I've made a new friend, perhaps even been quasi-adopted by a new family, these creative and loving and giving Coluccis. They fill me with their love and their stories. Empty garage, full heart.

OCTOBER 14, 2017
A Dream

I dreamt this morning that Tommy came back. I told Jordan before class this morning that I had woken up before dawn and then went back to half sleep and had this vivid dream. "You can't call that a dream, then, if you weren't really sleeping. That's just pure consciousness," he said.

So, dream or not, Tommy came back. There had been some kind of mistake and he wasn't really dead. We were at home, but it was a new house and lots of people were there. Some were cooking. I didn't know them well, but they were getting ready to make an involved meal in the kitchen that hadn't yet been set up. We were so glad to see him, of course, but also confused. He felt the same way, like of course he was glad to be alive, but it was confusing. He wondered if he should have started walking west instead of coming home to us. He started helping to set up the kitchen. I was worried about him and told him to just rest, because he looked terrible. He was bloated and needed a haircut. A haircut, I thought; is the barbershop in Needham open today? I think so, it's Saturday. There's always a line; better get there fast.

The alarm went off and I hit snooze, resting in that in-between place. I see Tommy walking across the room, tall, strong, lean, naked, sweet. He left this earth at his prime. Not his physical prime, I guess, but as his whole self, a beautiful soul in a beautiful body. My friend April came last week and spent the night. Her mother had died on May 11. Over the summer, she went to Cuba after the funeral to connect with her mother's family. The ladies who sang at church there practice the Santería religion. "Don't cry for your mother," they told her. "That keeps her tied to the earth. Let her go in peace."

These tears I cry, are they holding him back? Am I holding on to him too much and not setting him free? Am I wrong to say that I would give anything to have him back? What was this dream of his returning, uncomfortable, ill at ease, unsure, confused? Of course, he cannot come back. But does that also mean that I have to let him go, to stop crying and holding him to earth? Maybe it's time, my friend; maybe it's time.

6

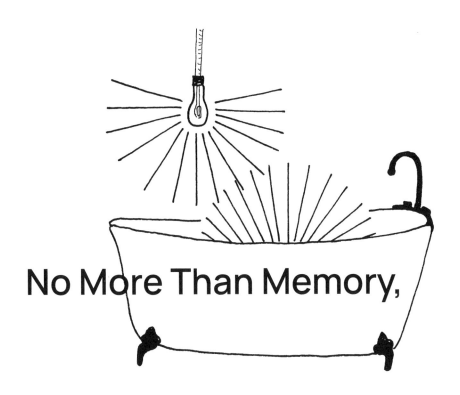

No More Than Memory,

Love's Afterglow?

OCTOBER 23, 2017
Palimpsest

As soon as my Uber arrives from the airport to the Campo di Fiori in Rome, Kathryn says we are leaving for Civita, an ancient Etruscan town. My best friend from graduate school and Sophie's godmother, she is in Rome teaching for the month. Her husband and kids are at home in the US, with their busy lives; they have come with her before, but not this time. We made this plan back in May. "I will be in Rome for the month of October; you must come," she said.

I am not sure exactly when Kathryn arrived at my house after Tommy died; it may have been that first night, or perhaps the second. Sophie called her and then she was on a plane, she was in my house, she was there. Over those first days, so many friends arrived from close and far, coming to do the many things that needed doing. Lisa came from Providence, Kathryn from Seattle, Amee from DC—"the clipboard ladies," someone called them. Amee taking down names, gifts, presents, arrivals, who sent the flowers. I have those lists, so incredibly long, and had every intention of writing thank-yous, but that hasn't happened yet.

Lisa was a friend from childhood; I knew Kathryn from grad school and Amee from Maine. It was like a dream to have these women, and many more, from different parts of my life, together. It seemed like they all must know each other, but of course, soon they did. Everyone had a job and it was a team effort. Kathryn brought her design and production skills, planning the service, designing the program and the prayer card, finding the songs and poems, sifting ideas, writing the obituary, getting the perfect photo of Tommy—on the beach on Nantucket, at his happiest on earth, the six children and us, the way it was supposed to be.

Come to Rome, she said, just come. But by the time fall came, I hesitated. However many months had gone by, Rome seemed faraway and unlikely. I was back at work with the busy fall madness, the girls at home with their high school pressure. But then, we are so lucky to have a new roommate in the Scarab (remember the boarding house). Sedi's full name, Lesedi, which means light in her mother's native Setswana, fits her perfectly. She brings freshness and energy into our grieving home. She will watch the kids while I travel for work, or to Rome, and everything seems possible again. "Go, Mom, go!" Liv urges, and I make my plan.

We would eventually see Rome, but first Kathryn and I are off to Civita, with its ten permanent residents and medieval architecture rising up like a volcanic island in a sea of farmland and brush—magnetic, precarious, precious. Kathryn could not wait to bring me here, to her spiritual home. She first came as a student with the heroine of our story, Astra Zarina, and Astra's husband, Tony, who together set up a campus for the University of Washington's architecture program both in Rome and in the incomparable hill town Civita di Bagnoregio. Astra was the first female in the fellows program at the American Academy of Rome in 1960. A beauty and a force of nature, her death in 2008 after forty years together left Tony grieving, living quietly in this place they restored and loved together.

We arrive after dark and park at the lot outside town. No cars allowed; it would be impossible to drive one if they were. A footbridge, with room for an emergency golf cart, connects the hill town to the mainland, and we walk across the bridge at night, the lights of the town sparkling and the sea below completely black. The footprint bridge has been rebuilt many times over the years, and I'm grateful for its stability. At night, the town is nearly empty. The piazza, the church, the town hall. Tourists pay a fee to enter the town, which is like a museum. This tiny town has rescued itself from certain death.

Kathryn cannot wait to show me around, and as soon as we have greeted Tony, we start our tour of the garden and the *sala grande*, the various rooms where we will stay. Her friends have already arrived and the unmistakable smell of dinner welcomes us. They are making one-pot chicken, a sumptuous chicken dish with caramelized onions, tomato sauce, almonds, and raisins served with polenta. I cannot remember the last time I had such a delicious meal.

Over the weekend we will roam the town, making the loop at different times of day to appreciate it. The others go on a day trip, but Kathryn and I stay, our conversation of twenty years picking up where it left off— fluid, direct, open, sometimes challenging. We are similar, the two of us, and we can push and relax, talk and listen; we can be strident and we can change our minds. We have lunch with Tony at his daily lunch spot. He sits with Sandro, who also lost his wife in the last few years, and we sit at the table next to them with a photographer who has just arrived in Civita for a monthlong fellowship, her tripod and large-frame camera in tow. She has brought 120 sheets of film and has already made eight photographs to be processed in November in Florence.

I have brought Tommy with me in so many different ways. He has become my traveling companion of sorts, and I realize how precious this is. I love seeing the world with him in my heart ("your heart, I carry it in my heart"); it makes me more wondrous, more grateful. But I also have this precious time with Kathryn, to share and grieve with her.

Tony comes and goes on his own clock, his schedule fairly well estab-lished—light breakfast and feeding the cats, lunch with Sandro at Alma Civita, afternoon rest, writing, managing his affairs, light dinner, opera on the radio, bed. But he joins us one night, bringing a story he has written about Astra. He hands it to Kathryn and asks her to read it to us.

We laugh out loud many times during the story, and for a moment I wish my stories were funny. We laughed out loud at the funeral, belly laughs; thank you, Joe Brooks! But my stories make people cry!

I am charmed by this love-filled man tearing up as Kathryn reads, just a spillover of moisture for a minute, not longer. Two thousand eight, I think; that's nine years. Yes, love is love. I know this; the love and the grief, neither ends; the laughter and the tears. And I hope that he has written more; so many stories to tell, such a rich life lived by this fearless, beautiful, perhaps brash woman.

On our way out of town, after stopping to say goodbye to Tony and Sandro at their lunch table, we find Astra's gravesite. As simple as possible, white Carrera stone, engraved in a modern typeface, with her name and year of birth and death, no dates other than the year: ASTRA ZARINA 1929 2008. Always looking for connection, I remark to Kathryn that 1929 was the year Katharine Lee Bates died. Astra picked up the narrative thread with her birth.

There may be no better treat than to be introduced to your friend's pas-sions. Back in Rome, I get to see the underground arches and artifacts of

the Theatre of Pompeii, the legendary site Kathryn researched for the graduate thesis she wrote in 1999 while we were in school at the University of
Virginia. I tour the Campo di Fiore and its buildings, home to her twenty-
year-old self and many selves since. She gives me history lessons and takes
me through the studio, introducing me to her students.

And for the two days I have in Rome, it is my place. I am filled with joy.
Remember that feeling, Katie—of joy so deep in your bones, in your stride,
in the pleasure of Rome, the pleasure of walking the city on a sunny day, a
little bit lost, stopping into every open church, because why wouldn't you?

I love being home in Bohemia, at home with my girls, but I love being
out in the world too. When I am in cities faraway, new landscapes, I think
of Tommy differently, and I think of my future differently. I am optimistic
and in motion. "Let's go, baby," and I think I am living our life still. So much
has changed, seemingly everything has changed, and yet. This was us, this
is us, there are many us-es, ourselves and the people we love.

OCTOBER 24, 2017
So Handsome

I buy a jacket and scarf just minutes before I have to get packed and leave
for the airport. That was not my intention. I was shopping, but for a purse.
"Enjoy Rome and then buy a handbag," my colleague Toni said. Because
she lost her mother this past year, I take her words to heart—treat yourself.

But as I walked down the Via Del Pellegrino, a leather coat in the window stops me in my tracks. Not a jacket, more of a coat, coming down to
the top of my thighs, covering my seat at a hockey game.

For Christmas last year, I bought Tommy a European-style Barbour
coat. I loved shopping for him, feeling all the pleasure I do not take in
shopping for myself. It may be the best purchase I have ever made in my
life. I would call it a gift, in that every time he wore it, he felt like a gift to
me. It is black with a wax finish and chunky silver hardware. On Tommy it
was like hand in glove, butter on bread. He was so handsome I would feel
my heart bursting with pride, utter delight in him. In my mind, he will be

forever crossing the rink, one rink or another, coming over to the stands where I stand with the parents, this gorgeous man, looking for me, smiling at me, this jacket somehow making him princely.

Last year, I determined to finally buy a new winter parka. All these years in Boston and I still hate the cold, but why, oh why, do I not have proper gear? Too vain, perhaps. I know this coat will not be the winter coat I need. But it is absolutely the winter coat I want. If I could wear his coat, I would, but his 6-foot, 2-inch frame makes that simply impossible. Still, I make sure it is at the front of his closet, just so I know it is there.

Inside the store on the Via Del Pellegrino, I really don't think I am going to buy it (funny how the mind can make the plausible impossible), but the salesperson tells me to just try it on, and I do. Its fit and feel is so perfect that I cannot take it off. I wear it in the store for minutes, many minutes slipping by. I am supposed to be packing, getting to the airport; I cannot buy it but I cannot take it off. She tells me I can get money back for taxes at the airport. She shows me beautifully crafted gloves and boots, which tempt me not at all but are a willing distraction to allow the inevitability of the coat purchase to sink in.

Can I be him in this coat? When I walk to the train in my spiffy jacket, will I feel like he felt? Will it possibly be warm enough to wear to the rink? The salesperson brings out scarves, showing me how to be just so, as in Italy. I cannot wear wool, and out she comes with a silk scarf in whites and grays. She ties it on me just so, and I look the part. She says it is the monkey, and I take off the scarf and see that the pattern is an abstraction of a monkey holding up his center finger. What? This beautiful handcrafted item is also a giant F-U monkey finger. I love it so much I want to cry. I buy both.

NOVEMBER 3, 2017
Flagpole

Writing feels harder these days; the articulation of what I am feeling and thinking feels like it is better left unsaid, unfelt. The acute pain has been dulled, muted. I don't wake up crying; I can breathe. But the distance also has another effect: perspective makes the magnitude of the loss clearer, and the sadness seems to have lodged so deeply inside me that I worry it is here to stay.

My loss, our loss, the world's loss.

The Quincy YMCA erected a flagpole in Tommy's honor, and we are here for the dedication. The incredible staff and board of the Y represent just another group of people whose lives he touched deeply. Again and again I hear the same thing—his kindness, brilliance, enthusiasm, natural grace, empathy, leadership. To see this gorgeous new building, with its 21,000 members, is to be reminded, again, that the world was a fundamentally better place for Tommy being in it.

The staff and board tell the story of Tommy walking in for his first interview. The Quincy Y was first opened in 1892, Bates and Coman's era, and had in recent years been housed in a dilapidated building with apartments upstairs, a model that had become antiquated. They had 8,000 members and needed a new building. The town of Quincy was experiencing its own moment of revitalization with the new high school and spruced-up downtown, all in view from the Y's front door.

I can see Tommy Niles walking into his interview. The South Shore YMCA had put out a Request for Proposals for development companies to act as their project manager or owners' rep for the Quincy Y renovation. This was not just another job for Tommy. Sports had always been a central part of his life, and he played Little League baseball and Pop Warner football. He'd told me the story of his freshman year of high school. After his father died, he went a little off the rails. He stopped playing sports, wore a trench coat, and avoided a lot of his usual friends. The good news is that he started to get involved in other things. He could juggle, and this got him a part in the school play. He met different kids; an older girl took an interest in him and invited him to theater parties.

But one day, after Tommy had missed football tryouts, he walked into the locker room, long hair, trench coat and all. The coach looked up and simply said, "Niles, get dressed." No questions, no hoops to jump through. He never looked back, and sports stayed a part of his core forever.

So, when it was time for the Y to make their selection, the board members said their choice was easy. Tommy was connected to their mission. He brought a vast array of experience on projects of much-larger scale, but somehow the Y team always felt like they had his full attention. He had also priced his proposal competitively—half, perhaps, making the choice even easier. They didn't know then that after working for a fee for three years, he would work the next three as a volunteer.

The calls, cards, and words keep coming. So many people, so many stories. I have to summon all my energy to allow myself to feel the joy, pride, and majesty of him without immediately feeling sliced by despair. Living with his glory but without him is not easy. Describing the dull thud is not easy either; there's no poetry in dull, no lyricism in sludge, no future to be bright.

NOVEMBER 11, 2017

Logan

Walking through the double doors to the lobby at Terminal C, I feel dread creeping over me. It's like I can see him standing in that soaring lobby space, watching for me. How many times was he there waiting? A few dozen? More?

His face, sometimes square jawed, sometimes angular, depending the moment. Coming toward me, after I hadn't seen him for almost any period of time, he'd be square jawed, full frontal. This is how he will break my heart every time as I see him coming across the rink, through the airport, waiting on Boylston. This is his party face, newly shaven after a visit to the barbershop, clean and neat and movie-star handsome. His angular side is more intimate, perhaps tired, less prepared for the world. This angular face is driving or doing the crossword. I would reach out and touch his face, all of it, registering the temperature, the elasticity of his skin, the edge of his jaw and cheekbone. I touched him, always my right hand, cupped, the left side of his face in my hand, resting there a moment, soaking in his aspect.

But this day it is as if he is actually waiting, and I know exactly where, even though he was certainly never in the same spot more than once. I am walking through the lobby; I can't just stop, can I? I would always stop, a kiss and a long hug, but I have to keep moving, right? So the whole world doesn't know I have lost my mind. As if on a dare to myself, I walk straight through him, and I am sure I feel him. I am losing my mind; it's confirmed. I watched his heart stop, delivering no more oxygen to his brain, pumping no more blood to animate his limbs. I saw his body refuse his beautiful mind the ability to think, speak, express itself. I may have even seen his soul linger there, hovering, but maybe that is just my imagination, now having read perhaps too many accounts of near-death experiences.

This is what they mean by incarnation—this soul with this mind in this body, each somehow distinct and yet indivisible, dependent on each other, and uniquely combined to create this person. All of our experiences and influences that dominate our daily perspective—family, education, the stories we tell about ourselves, our desires for our children—pale in comparison to the miracle of this soul, this mind, this body, uniquely combined to make this man, this woman, this child.

Is it possible that nearly all of what we obsess about in our everyday life falls into one bucket that could only be love? Love is the animation of life in action, the expression of the miracle of this temporary symbiosis. I am in awe that this version of mind, body, and soul could come together on this earth, at this time, and express itself through our love.

NOVEMBER 12, 2017
Romantic Piha

There were a lot of complications with our flights to New Zealand. It was a miracle that we flew there together, next to each other. He wanted so badly to fly home together, but it just wasn't realistic. How did he know that every second mattered? As it turns out, during our relationship we spent many more hours apart than together. And yet, we were together all the time, it seemed, whether physically proximate or not. This is part of what is now confusing.

My flight left Auckland around 1 p.m. on Sunday, April 2, 2017, and his left at 7 p.m. that night. He parked the rental car at the Auckland airport and walked me inside, as if we were at Logan. I checked in and he stood in line with me right up until security. The vacation was over. It had indeed been a honeymoon, and neither of us wanted to break the cone of intimacy. The whole trip was magical, but the last night was a fantasy come true. We had been on the Coromandel Peninsula but wanted to go see the black beaches at Piha, and we booked a last-minute house named Romantic Piha, on the cliffs overlooking the beach.

We went to the beach first, of course, following Tommy's goal to bathe in every body of water we visited. It was late afternoon when we got there, and the tide was out. Miles of fine, black sand stretched in every direction, just an inch of water skimming the surface. We stopped for pizza and beer at a restaurant near the beach, a surfer town. We figured that once we went home, there would be nowhere to go.

The house was like a Hollywood set. You drove down a long driveway and parked away from the house, walking up a hill to a wood-sided ranch house. Stepping inside at the front door, you could see straight through to the back over a large deck; there was not a single soul or house to be seen in the panoramic view, just this incredible expanse over a tangle of green to the ocean, with a cacophony of insects humming loudly.

We could not have planned it better, this last night, but of course we hadn't planned it. Our journey had been like that. We followed our own rhythm, luck, and directions from friends and strangers, somehow ending up at what was perhaps the most romantic place on earth for our last night in New Zealand.

We had brought a bottle of red wine, and we sat on the couch on the edge of this earth. We made love there on the couch and I fell asleep, waking in the middle of the night to see Tommy staring out over the expanse. He felt so calm and satisfied; this trip had been so right. Life was so right.

We thought we would come back here with the Robustellis, renting this house and the one next door for a few nights to enjoy this magical place with friends. This trip would be the first of many. There were so many places to go, and to travel together would be the supreme pleasure of his life, he said. "Take me to . . ." Paris, above all, but South America, Africa, Australia—let's go everywhere.

This was Tommy's first cross-world trip. Invited for work, I had traded my first-class ticket for two coach, and we turned three nights of hotel rooms into nine. He was in heaven. For once, he didn't have to do it all; he could tag along as the spouse, the plus one. The future was unfolding before him—a partnership, an adventure, a new phase of life.

When it was time to fly home, I went through security and he went to return the rental car and find a bar to watch Sunday sports. Characteristically, his adventure continued. He watched rugby on TV, and an hour after the first game ended, in walked the opposition team, and then the All-Blacks in their matching joggers. I was in the air, but he was in heaven, surrounded by this foreign culture of familiarity. All in uniform, they now surrounded him, laughing and joking, and of course he joined in their banter.

I still have the geeky compression socks he got us for that flight. I am wearing them now, flying alone across the ocean to Cape Town. (We're going to Cape Town, baby, I say in my mind, wondering for the thousandth time if I am crazy.) I don't know why I wear these god-awful socks except that he got them and said to wear them, so I do. It's raining during the lay-over in Paris. Don't worry, baby, we're just passing through. It looks cold, rainy, and gray out there at Charles de Gaulle. We'll come back another time; this trip is to Cape Town. (Is it possible that you never went to Paris? How could you have died without ever going to Paris?)

How did he know then that he had to swim in every body of water? How did he know how completely precious it all was? I look at the photos he took on his phone—hundreds, literally, of me. I have photos of him too, and many photos of us together, mostly selfies. I have pictures of the gorgeous landscape from across the north and south islands. But he took hundreds of me from every angle. As in love with the landscape as he was, he was in love with me more. As I was in love with him.

Although New Zealand was amazing, we were the trip, it turns out. We went so faraway to be alone together. When I think about traveling with Tommy now, I understand the importance of time away. Our lives together at home were connected and communicative, but we did our big work while we were away, during periods of extended time in each other's presence, when a conversation could play out over hours and days. I learned that no flight is too long. Who cares? he said. We are on this plane together; the longer the better. Just wear your socks and drink water—his answer to all things, really.

I am grateful for every minute we had, but it also doesn't even feel like the time together is what defined us. We were together when we weren't together ("tug"), and now that he is not physically with me, I know that the essence of what made us Us is still making us Us in some way. Oh, God, how I want to fold time into quarters and slip in a moment together through a crease. It feels possible, but somehow just out of my reach. If I really focus, could I do it? Maybe if I cross enough time zones I can reverse time, like we gained and lost whole days coming and going to New Zealand; time is nothing but a construct.

And so I go. I have my beautiful oyster shell necklace and my hideous compression socks, and I go. I just say yes. No flight is too long, no trip not worth taking. Come on baby, let's go.

NOVEMBER 17, 2017
Half a Year

Who is the person with whom you can learn? Maybe that is the definition of love. We were so busy learning about so many things—about love, about calm, about pleasure. We were learning about family and how to fully enjoy the present. We were developing habits together; we were practicing being ourselves. We were learning to live in this new way, as our best, most comfortable selves.

We hadn't gotten around to thinking about death or dying. Sure, we had started to make plans. We talked to my parents about what would happen with the house if something happened to me, how to structure my will so that you could stay there with the girls. We worked with your insurance broker to set up wills and trusts if something happened to you. But that was all academic, a question of if, not when. We didn't really believe that something would happen because we were busy living. And so, we did that poorly. We had started but we didn't finish. We had an idea that we would have our affairs in order by the time of our wedding on July 22. We even thought we were above average to have this foresight. Almost counts only in horseshoes and hand grenades. We were preparing, but we weren't ready, financially or legally. There was no clarity around wills and money, no legal structure to execute what you would have wanted.

But what about spiritually? Were you ready for your death? Did living through your parents' deaths prepare you? Did you understand grief? As you nursed and juiced for Andy Mac, did you watch his death, wondering about the physical and spiritual aspects? Did you develop an idea about what it meant for you?

The first thing Andrew Colucci did when he came to the house was to scour the bookshelves. He had sent you a book about reincarnation that he was eager to discuss with you, but he didn't know if you had read it. He was immediately concerned for your spiritual life, wishing that you two had delved into that conversation about the only thing that really matters now. Despite the many ideas and books you shared, the two of you never talked about that one.

You and I didn't discuss it either. You had a worksheet in your drawer, with five questions about preparing for death, and we had planned to answer them together. I read aloud passages of *When Breath Becomes Air* and *Being Mortal* beside you in bed, crying while doing so. But we were focused on living and loving. It was so deliriously attractive that we hadn't yet made time to talk about death.

And yet, is it possible that we are doing this together too? It feels like it to me, most days. I am so grateful for your guidance.

I know now, as we get some distance and understanding, that I am learning about life and death with you just as I learned about love and life with you. We are in this journey together still. I hope and pray that you are progressing on yours, and I promise that I will do my best to help, as you have helped me. That as much as you are here teaching me, I am somehow teaching you too. We can do this together too, my love, unbound by the ties of the material, free.

NOVEMBER 23, 2017
Thanksgiving

It's good to have a baby around. I tell the girls that baby Emma is coming to Thanksgiving dinner, and the whole energy changes. At dinner, each of them angles to sit next to her and her parents. Emma is, of course, also "our baby." Her parents had been planning to come over in February to watch the Super Bowl (the best Super Bowl in the history of mankind, that is). Tommy had the projector set up and prepared a full spread to watch the game on the big wall in Bohemia.

But then we got word that Meagan and Dave were headed to the hospital, the makings for her appetizer left on the kitchen counter. The miracle baby was born at the exact moment of the kickoff—a good omen, no doubt. The Patriots were down 0–21 at the half, 3–28 in the third. Tommy had promised the girls that if the Patriots won, he would take them to Dick's to get Super Bowl victory shirts. And of course that's just what they did. Edelman's catch, White's touchdown, then Amendola's; our hero, Tom Brady, leading the team to win 34–28. Tommy and I sat in bed and watched the highlights for weeks, reliving the game. And Emma came home from the hospital, perfect sweetness, our first grandchild of sorts.

Watching her parents, I'm reminded of the experience of being a new parent. Your baby is so perfect that you want to bottle up their goodness and deliciousness. You think every stage is the best one. You cannot imagine their future, and already you have forgotten their past because they fill the present so completely. But of course, even though you want them to stay this way forever, their perfectness replenishes daily, monthly, and each new phase is the most wonderful one. After they have lost their baby fat, or can say their l's and r's, you would never send them back in time. You only ever want them to move forward in their development.

Yoga class was sold out in advance this holiday morning. Tara taught masterfully, open hearted and sweaty, room filled to capacity. She played "Landslide," one of the songs Tommy taught me to sing while driving through New Zealand. "Well, I've been afraid of changin'/'Cause I've built my life around you / But time makes you bolder / Even children get older / And I'm getting older, too." I started crying early today, a dark room, sweat and tears indistinguishable. I go to this last place Tommy lived on earth to be with him, honor him, mourn him, love him. I often cry there, but today it was almost like I got through the crying early, in the first warrior one series, so that I could get to the next place in my mind.

Now that I have gotten to this next place in my life, now that I know what death, grief, and loss is, would I wish to turn myself back? To what point? I think of my younger self, before I met Tommy and fell in love with him. The self who hadn't experienced love, not real love. Would I turn myself back to that self? And what about Tommy? Now that he has experienced his own death, who is to say he would turn that experience back? What knowledge, peace, understanding has he acquired over these last six months?

As I watch Emma, now sitting up so sprightly, knocking over the tower of blocks, eating her cooked vegetables and playing with the dogs, her face lighting up when I walk into the room and erupting in pleasure when she sees one of the girls, I know that I cannot turn back this moment of evolution in our lives.

The truth is that Tommy was always ahead of most of us. A child who understood, "It just comes easy to me." A son who could say, "I got enough." A grownup who had enough love for everyone. A man who led with kindness to a degree that changed people's perceptions of themselves and the world around them. Perhaps it is not surprising that he is ahead of us now.

So today I am deeply thankful for the tremendous gifts he gave us in his life, and yes, what he has given us even in his death. I never fathomed the expanse of the universe or the depths of love until now, had no idea of the mystery and wonder of life, had not pondered the meaning and material of death. Can I handle the seasons of my life? Only with your help, my love.

NOVEMBER 26, 2017
Sad News from the Scarab

Sad news today. I was invited for tea at the home of two retired Wellesley High School teachers, Jeanie and Brooks Goddard. My friends Karen and Mike Buckley suggested I meet them to talk about writing.

Jeanie and Brooks live in a brown-shingled house in Needham. I felt like I was in the Scarab of yore—the house is filled with reminders of their travels, like the Bates-Coman house. Sculpture, art, fabric, tapestries—it was incredible to be in a living room that felt like what I imagined Bates's studio to feel like at the Scarab. The southern sun beat in the front window, making the living room warm and toasty. There was tea, pistachios, and cider donuts. My hosts were so present, leaning forward, eager to learn, listen, talk, share, suggest. This must be what it was like to visit with Bates, the closest I may come.

But then an unexpected sadness. When talk turned to the Bates house, I learned that Jeanie and Brooks had known the Robinsons' daughter, Carolyn. The period of time when the Robinsons owned the house—1960 to 2004—is vague in the house's history. I knew from the tax records that Walter was an engineer and Muriel was an artist and teacher. The city directory does not list children, although I had a vague recollection that they had some. According to the records, they also had boarders, at least through 1966.

Their daughter, Carolyn, was a Wellesley High School student (class of 1972). Tragic beyond belief, she died in high school of stomach cancer. I can hardly breathe; how can this be real? What child dies of stomach cancer? How is it that children die? I think quite differently now of the Robinsons, parents surviving the loss of their daughter.

Jeanie brings out a 1971 yearbook. Carolyn is the tall blond in the back row. Her friend wrote a poem about her that appeared in the 1972 yearbook. Jeanie will find it tomorrow at school, this beautiful poem that they both remember forty-five years later.

I guess every house has a history. Every house has been a backdrop for many lives and deaths. Every house has ghosts. When April was here last month, she marveled at the Scarab's long history. Where she grew up in the

Bronx, all the houses have been burned or torn down, bought up, redeveloped. She has been researching and reviving her story, through stories and photographs and archives, but the architecture is gone now. I am grateful for this house and its stories, but sad, too, for the recognition that this thing we call life is also full of loss—early, tragic loss no less. The Scarab was aptly named—there is no reincarnation, no rebirth, without death.

DECEMBER 2, 2017

What Does Love Look Like in a Yellow Vest?

The mystery of the compression socks is solved. Why had Tommy come home with ugly black matching compression socks that day? So many things to get done, but that was top of his list. We would fly to San Francisco and then board another plane for the seventeen-hour flight to Auckland. When we got on the first plane, he broke out the socks right away. Having made many cross-country flights, I thought it was overkill, but he had insisted.

I meet two of Tommy's colleagues for lunch in Providence, Aleita and Maria. They want to talk about Tom, as they called him—about the last time they saw him, their last communication with him, about that day before and what the hell happened. About how they admired him, enjoyed him, miss him.

One has a blended family with lots of interpersonal and financial complexity. She and her husband just put their house into both of their names—you know, "in case something happens." They are writing their wills, getting things sorted out. The other also speaks about her husband, tears in her eyes. She says, "I think about you so often, about Tom, about your relationship. My husband is an amazing father and a great man, but I appreciate him more now. When he wants to make love—in the old days I may have said no—I think of you and I say yes. I think it's brought us closer."

I am glad for these small lessons in love and respect and being a couple, and how love and respect materialize in all sorts of ways—the way we treat each other in that intimate moment, the way we secure and protect each other—you know, just in case.

And I learn from Aleita that it was her insistence that made Tommy buy the socks. I had met her briefly once before at the South Street Landing jobsite. Bill Clinton had come to do a stump speech for Hillary in March 2016, and Sophie and I went down to Providence to hear him. Aleita was the project manager on the site and wore a yellow vest and hardhat.

I told Aleita that it takes hundreds of people to make a project like this happen. No, she says, it took Tom. Hundreds of people are involved, sure; they have their interests, their contributions, their demands, but without Tom at the center making everything somehow hang together, no way.

At least 6 feet tall, she is close to Tommy's height. They are like twins, I think. I'd heard so much about her—his partner and nemesis, the one across the table, the two of them navigating every detail, change order, delay, and complaint. I knew how much he cared about her, and I imagined that she felt the same. I had seen her sitting near the front in a side pew at the funeral but hadn't heard from her until about a month ago.

Six months and counting, yet giant tears flowed from her eyes, whole and magnifying as they cascaded down her cheeks. She had warned me. She'd lost a few people close to her recently but doesn't quite know why she can't get over Tom. He made an immediate impression when they met in October 2015 to discuss contracts for the parking garage. "Who is that?" she thought. They jousted, fought, conspired, and laughed during those two years, and when he was going on that trip to New Zealand, she panicked. People die from blood clots on those long plane rides. She's still worried that the flight may have caused his death. I don't think so, I ventured, and she was relieved to hear that he wore his compression socks, both ways.

I don't know why she was so worried about him back in March, and she doesn't either. She may not even have realized how much she cared for him until he was dead. He was just a colleague, after all. Love, I say, comes in many forms. She dismisses it, uncomfortable with that word, but I know how much Tommy loved her. He talked about her, would be frustrated with her, was hopeful for her, wanted her to do more with her career. She says they had the kind of relationship where they could make things work.

I think of the million times I have quoted Peter Senge, MIT professor, Buddhist, philosopher, teacher, writer. All meaningful work happens through collaboration. Collaboration is based on relationships. The quality of the relationships defines the quality of the collaboration and in turn defines the resulting work. Senge talks about work being produced by "networks of loving relationships." What does love have to do with work? I learned from him that love is allowing the other to be a legitimate other. It's about respecting that the other person is a whole person and allowing for their wealth of perspective and experience, understanding their flaws and strengths as you understand your own. So, love and work are inseparable.

I know how much Tommy loved his work. Loved it. Making buildings, making projects, running teams, people, people, people. And I know for a fact that Tommy loved Aleita. He just cared more. I know, I heard. And here she is, with these contact-lens-size tears rolling down her face. "Do you know how many genuine people you meet in your life?" she asks, "especially in this business?" He was truly one of a kind.

DECEMBER 23, 2017

Atta Way, Kid

From my usual place in the stands, I watch Bliss's feet move back and forth nervously while the national anthem plays, not very loud and a little scratchy, but reverent nonetheless. It's the third ice hockey game of the season, a Friday home game against our biggest rival, first night of winter break, and Bliss's name is announced as a starter. Liv and her cousin Phoebe are captains; Bliss is playing center on Phoebe's line, and Liv is on defense. It's like a dream come true, and it's impossible to fathom that Tommy is not here—this is his moment as much as anyone's. Except that, of course, he is here. I can feel him next to me in the stands; I can see him, hear him cheering and whistling for the girls. "Atta way, kid!" "Let's go, Bebe!" So full of pride and pleasure, his presence palpable.

The puck drops and Bliss wins the faceoff; the fantasy is now in motion. Two minutes in, Phoebe, Bliss, and Bridget get the puck deep in their zone, Phoebe passes the puck to Bliss, and with an explosion from heaven, Bliss scores. I burst into tears. The outrageous pride, the fierce pleasure, the knowledge, finally, that he is here and deeply a part of us. This was his dream; he saw it all for us—Bliss, me, Sophie, and Liv. Our future was his dream, and he will live it through us.

Earlier this afternoon, the snow started to fall past the windows in Bohemia, dusk coming early with the gray sky. A magical feeling, the end of school, the start of Christmas, the snow, the big game tonight. I had gotten a voicemail earlier in the day from a publisher. My collaborator, Harry Connolly, and I have been working on a book called *Design with Love: At Home in America*, a tribute to the diversity, beauty, and passion of the America we have had the pleasure of getting to know through the Rose Fellowship over the past seventeen years. He is photographing and I am writing, telling stories of activists and organizers, designers and architects, builders and leaders from all over the country—border communities, tribal communities, big-city neighborhoods, and small towns. Despite an image of a divided red-blue country, despite the wall and the horror of separation, the America we know is rich in kindness and thrives in the diverse cultures that are unique to its identity.

I pace Bohemia, talking about this book idea, and we talk about affordable housing design and development. The editor is all in; this is the book we need, she says. As I walk, I open the gauzy curtains all the way and let myself perceive the snow globe I am in, as if the world has been shaken and I am moving through the snow falling all around me. "How white the flakes come down, like the thoughts of God," Katharine Coman said while lying in Bohemia, preparing for her death. Here now, my eyes are caressed by the visual reminders of our world: The endless piles of books stacked everywhere. Tommy's beautiful gray-leather couch, his soft calfskin chairs, my deep-orange chairs, and all the pieces of art and memory, our lives brought together so beautifully in harmony.

I walk toward the art wall, the eight dancing figures spinning and jumping, asking and suggesting unknown possibilities, and pace back and forth down the 20-foot timeline of the Scarab.

"I have another book," I say to the editor, "only this one is nearly written." It's the Friday before the holiday weekend, but she has all the time in the world. "Tell me about it." She's passionate about architecture, so I start with the house and the history of its original owners, what they have taught me over my time here, how I learned about love and death and grief with them, up here in Bohemia. I tell her about our hero and the magical gift of his life. "Send it to me," she says, "I would love to read it."

As I walk and talk, my heart is bursting with the feeling of something new, something so right, the making manifest of the future I knew was there but couldn't see. Tommy could see it; he could always see my future. He could see that my present and my future had to be the fullest expression of me, and if I did that, it would be beautiful and meaningful. I just have to have the faith in myself that he had in me.

After the game, Bliss makes herself a burrito in the kitchen and we talk about the game. I told her I cried and how I felt Tommy next to me the whole time. She tells me that she knows, of course she knows. She talks to him, and tonight, as her skates glided back and forth in what looked like nervousness, she was meditating and talking to him during the anthem. She has done it. She has brought his love into herself as fuel; he is hers forever.

Tommy taught me about love, and then he taught me about grief. But now I realize that what he really taught me was about the bodily feeling of gratitude. My heart has never been so full, so open. We get to keep his outrageous generosity and kindness. We get to keep his vision for us to be fully ourselves, and the knowledge that there is nothing more loving than wishing that for another human soul.

What I didn't understand then was that this writing was my way of being in conversation with Tommy. "Have I not sometimes felt your presence nigh?" You said, "I will not leave you comfortless." Sometimes the writing felt automatic, and there are parts of it I don't remember writing, our endless conversation cut short abruptly, impossibly. I find his voice in the darkness of the yoga studio, in the depth of my dreams, in my keyboard in Bohemia. If I am quiet enough, sometimes I can make out the words.

This is the gift he gave us, and we are now ready to fully receive it.

7

Your Sentence

by My Quavering Voice

Was Told

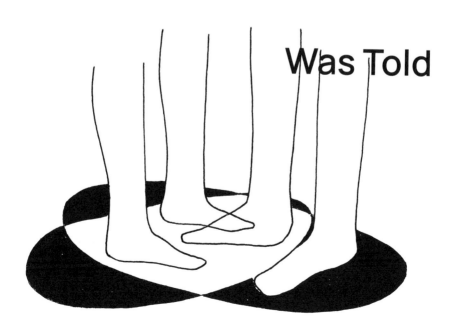

DECEMBER 31, 2017
Begin Again

I may be nearly done with this year, but sadly I am not "done." It's a panicky feeling. I did a good job, I thought, of getting through Thanksgiving and Christmas. More than getting through; actually enjoying it. We hosted seventeen for Thanksgiving, all family, and then fourteen for Christmas Eve, all friends. I went to a few parties; I shopped and wrapped and cooked. We got the tree up early and lights on the house. I thought it would be harder than it was. Christmas morning with the girls was warm and wonderful, and the day at my parents' house was lovely.

And then New Year's came. Two years ago we celebrated the new year in Sosua, Dominican Republic, with all the kids, the beginning of what we hoped would be our new family. The town went wild that night, and it was fun to be out on the streets at midnight. Last New Year's Eve, Tommy, always my biggest fan, came to hear me give a keynote to 800 architecture students in Boston. We went out for dinner and then back to the students' dance party.

It's not the night that's the problem, of course. It's the symbol. For me, 2017 will be the last year Tommy was alive. And that is a terrible thing to have in the past. The year 2017 was also perhaps the happiest I have been in my life, the half year where I felt happiness as a tangible object I held, a current of energy.

And then, of course, everything changed. Except that in some ways, it didn't. I experienced grief for the first time, perhaps the most powerful emotion I have ever felt. The depth of my love became increasingly apparent as the pain and anguish coursed through me. I was falling deeper and deeper in love. Writing gave me a portal into the depth of this remarkable man. My curiosity only grew, my admiration intensified. Is it like that for everyone? That after you are gone, those around you grow to love and respect you more? I don't know, but this new level of love is another hallmark of 2017.

What does it mean for this year to be over? It's not the year of magical thinking; it's not a year since his death. It's just the end of his last year on earth. The reality hardened, the fact immutable. The world moves on without him. But I hold him close still. I can see the beads of sweat on his face, clear as day, as if he is right there with me in yoga class. I hear him breathing gently, lying on his side in shavasana, my knees curled up, pausing before I sit up and begin again.

JANUARY 10, 2018

In Bohemia, Still

Have you seen this space? Have you sat with me and watched the sky change colors? It changes your worldview. Bohemia has a magical quality; it holds memory, yes, and ideas, and words written, but also beauty and creativity, softness and color.

It's a Tuesday morning in January, tons of snow outside, but on this first warm day the tension is loosening, streams of water flowing as the snow starts to melt off the roof. I make a coffee and sit, first at my work table and then on the leather couch, piles of books stacking up on the leather ottoman. Tommy insisted that the coffee table be soft; it's meant for feet to be put up on. I put my feet up.

The sunlight is streaming in behind me from the south, bathing the space in yellow light and warming my shoulders. The bed in its eastern nook was hastily made, but the matching side tables and lights are filled with photos, the boys as babies and kids on his side, the girls on mine. My table has books everywhere, on and below, but his is tidy, empty. The cardboard angel floats above my side of the bed—is she still looking out for me?

All the walls and ceiling are painted white, a Benjamin Moore color called Chantilly Lace. It sounds prissy, but it's a beautiful white, clear and bright, neither too blue nor too yellow, just perfect to give some shade and shadow to the walls and ceiling covered in ship lap, tracing the outline of the Scarab's structure. Pops of color are everywhere, warm orangey reds, golden yellows, and teal blues in the art—a Matisse print and Ben's outrageously delightful dancing figures. The needle on the record player is broken, and I cannot seem to fix it; it sits on midcentury-modern crenelated cabinets I got years ago at an antique store. A big IKEA table serves as my desk, with seven windows facing west providing the primary vista, up and out and across the sky.

In addition to the coffee (and wine) kitchen, Bohemia contains everything you need in a mini-apartment. In the north front of the house, we made a flow-through space for baths, laundry, closet, dressing room, all in sync with the rest of the room. The clawfoot tub that was original to the house found its perfect spot under the low north window.

It's hard for me to describe how happy this space makes me, or how complete.

This is the space we created and lived in together like it was made for us, which of course it was. As designers, we absolutely accomplished our goal. It embodies our vision for how to live. It makes you appreciate each moment; you cannot escape the presence of now in this room, with its ever-changing ribs and hull-like structure reflecting light to surround, lift, and comfort you.

Visit me in this space and enter my world. It's another country, this place where kindness is made physical and beauty is the platform. But beware, there may be tears.

FEBRUARY 1, 2018
Swenson! Niles!

I get to class early, something that happens more these days. I find a spot and lie down on the mat. Tommy's spot, on my left, is empty as Tara starts the class. But just as we begin, a man puts down his mat next to mine. He's in his mid-fifties, a nice-looking white guy with a shiny gold wedding ring and an easy way about him. Not a regular, but I've seen him before.

Tara turns the music up. I am feeling strong and limber these days. I've been working on my handstand and doing drop-backs to back bends like I did in my thirties. It feels good to be in training.

So many things feel good these days. There are external goodnesses. Liv gets into her first-choice college. Liv and Bliss's hockey team is on fire.

I am back to work and in my groove. I credit Tommy with this, as if he is the maker of all things good. "Thank you, Tommy," I find myself saying often. But I'm starting to notice something far more powerful. I notice the kindness in others more. Are they more attuned? Do they listen deeper than they used to? Is Tommy's spirit literally infecting the people around me? The world feels so incredibly generous right now that it seems like it has to be him.

As we get into the flow, the guy next to me is adding a round of push-ups between every vinyasa. The class is hot and hard, and I think, whew, pace yourself, but he's going for it. At some point over the past few months, it occurred to me that Tommy's last hour on earth was doing yoga. What would an ideal last hour be? *The Tibetan Book of Living and Dying* describes the process of death in detail and explains how to best prepare, through meditation, for one's death. "I have found that the easiest way to understand what is happening during the process of dying, with its outer and inner dissolution, is as gradual development and dawning of ever more subtle levels of consciousness," Rinpoche writes. It's hard to apply this meditative death to what I saw Tommy experience with the paramedics surrounding him. But as I imagine what he was experiencing during that last hour of class, I think I would like to have my last hour be on the yoga mat.

I feel the man moving next to me and I wonder, if this were his last hour on earth, would this be how he wanted to spend it? As class goes on, he runs out of steam a bit, all those push-ups, but he stays with it and we come to final resting pose. I want to ask him, like it's a research project. "Hey, what have you been thinking these last sixty minutes," as if he could shed some light on Tommy's experience. I keep that question to myself.

Class ends and I feel awkward about even thinking about this man's death, but he stands up and gives me a high five. There are people on all sides of us, but he is thanking me for a great class. "You really pushed it all the way through; you inspired me," he says. I resist my urge to overly thank him or share my thoughts and instead just say, "Have an awesome day; see you next time." And I know I will. It is not his moment to die; he needs to get showered and get to work.

As I walk out, Tara makes a quip about my being on time. "What's up with that, Swenson?" She's still expecting us to walk in late, tiptoeing our way through the bodies in motion to find a spot. "Swenson! Niles!" she'd call out, and still does in her mind.

FEBRUARY 5, 2018
Day to Night

The photographer Stephen Wilkes came to Enterprise's New York office. We are exploring whether we can use the power of photography, digital imaging, and predictive analytics to fundamentally change the way people perceive climate change, and take action to prevent it. He showed us a series of before-and-afters, hinting at strategies to convey the reality of climate change. But it was the day-to-night series that I cannot shake.

For each of the day-to-night images, set all over the world, Wilkes sets up his camera in one spot for more than twenty-four hours, during which he shoots a series of photos. He then edits them, showing the progression from sunrise to night and revealing all the activity in one image. One of the images is of a watering hole in Africa. Over the course of a day, dozens of different species of animals come to drink. Many are would-be predators or antagonistic to each other, and yet here they are, side by side in the edited images, sharing in their common interest. It's fascinating, really. It makes you see places and time differently.

I feel that flattening sometimes up in Bohemia. I feel like the space is a vessel for the activities that have taken place within it. It holds the people, their thoughts, the lives lived there. I think of Katharine Coman, working to finish her books before the cancer made that impossible. I feel comforted knowing that she lived her last months in Bohemia, knowing full well myself the peace that space exudes. Bates talks about her last months at the top of the still-busy household, monitoring the sounds of people coming and going, keeping track of the domestic nature of the house, as I do.

I feel the sacredness of the space. "In her hushed and shadowed Bohemia she lay, breathing more and more faintly, apparently at peace, still with her own dignity, her own reserve upon her, even in dying. The hand I was holding clasped mine closely, but not with any suggestion of distress. The last text, I repeated to her as she sank beyond the reach of human love, was the one she held, perhaps, most precious: 'Underneath are the everlasting arms.' She ceased breathing so gradually, so quietly, that we could not tell the instant—approximately half-past nine—when she entered a new life."

And then Katharine Lee Bates, living up here for fourteen more years, loving, mourning, writing, and moving forward. Did the dozens of short-term residents in the 1930s, '40s, and '50s feel the power of that room? Did it affect their lives? I found a stack of *Compton's Pictured Encyclopedias*, copyright 1922, inscribed by Polly Jackson in July 1944, so I can imagine her, too, reading these eight volumes of world history complete with color renderings and maps.

Today was a good day in Bohemia, Super Bowl Sunday. Dave came to set up the projector. Sedi came up the stairs periodically to check in about the chili and cornbread, and later to ruminate on her life choices, considering graduate school. Bliss overtook the table and laid out a week of homework. Liv came to watch *Tom versus Time*. Later, all of us gathered, and Meagan scampered after little Emma, who was crawling around the room. I can flatten time in my mind and Tommy is there, getting ready for the game, setting everything up, his anticipation and pleasure evident. And the four of us are there together, experiencing the thrill of the comeback and victory.

The space gives me this frame, like carefully curated photos on the wall. Only Bohemia is not a rectangular frame but more like a carved vessel, the earth curved in its view. Sunrise to sunset, year after year, many things get edited out, but the essentials remain: the crew working in October when the leaves outside were bright yellow and the room was filled with golden light, and the sound of saws. Tommy and I going upstairs to check on the day's progress when we got home from work, soaking in the possibilities, planning, making decisions. Tommy on the couch, working on his laptop, playing guitar. Leaning forward tying his shoes. The pink sunrise of May 17, Tommy walking across the space naked in his glory. Writing his obituary, one person after another coming to sit at the computer, editing, reading, refining. The kids and I planning his service, the seven of us plus Chrissie, Amee, and Lisa; the pastor coming; the friends coming to visit and sit with me. Lisa Neighbors coming to get the girls to school on a morning I could not get myself out of bed. The life lived, being lived, to be lived, all layered on top of each other, all captured in the frame, under the wings of the Scarab.

FEBRUARY 8, 2018
The Gentle Art of Swedish Death Cleaning

Sometimes lately, I find that I make decisions without remembering what prompted them. When *The Gentle Art of Swedish Death Cleaning* arrived from Amazon, I had some vague feeling that I had bought it but couldn't remember how I'd heard of it, what compelled me to purchase it, or even the act of doing so. My mind doesn't function the same as before, some details vivid but others hazy. Perhaps I need to death-clean my mind rather than my home. I assume now that I was attracted to the idea of death clean-ing as a practice. My hundred-year-old grandmother lives surrounded by her belongings, some with pieces of paper indicating which china goes to which grandchild. My father has begun to accumulate clothing, so that his multiple closets are overflowing and he has taken over the guest room. They do not seem concerned with the art of death cleaning.

Living with Tommy's leave-behinds has been a rare pleasure. I love hav-ing his objects around me, the everyday objects whose texture is wound into the fabric of my life. I tidied the front-hall closet last week and saw that his winter boots are still there on the shelves he made. I handed down the girls' too-small rain boots to the little girls down the street, but I left his boots. They are not hurting anyone.

The treasures and the treasure hunt have been one of the most reward-ing parts of this year: The finding, the learning, the wondering, the appre-ciating. Asking his friends or family about objects, some of which come with a story I never would have known. Putting together the pieces of the different stages of life. What does it mean to curate a life?

In *The Gentle Art of Swedish Death Cleaning*, the author conveys the importance of dealing with your own possessions so that someone else doesn't have to. But she also describes the joy of death cleaning for yourself. "One's own pleasure, and the chance to find meaning and memory, is the most important thing. It is a delight to go through things and remember their worth."

Last summer, Tommy's high school girlfriend, Chris, sent me a message: "The strangest thing just happened. I am at Keuka Lake working through the heart-wrenching task of sorting what is left of my parents' stuff and, after an hour or so of breathing dust and laughing at so many crazy family photos, I found an autographed photo of Ernie Davis (my dad coached him) and then a beautiful football portrait of Tommy that I didn't even remember seeing before. My dad loved him—they must be bonding now!"

Discovery and magic are sometimes in the mess. I guess you have to truly love someone to want to discover them, but when you do, the discovery makes your love that much deeper.

FEBRUARY 14, 2018
The Fellows Are Coming

Love takes many forms. I am not sure how I got so lucky to love my job as much as I do, for as long as I have, but I am grateful for this beautiful fact. The new class of Rose Fellows came to Boston last week. As tradition goes, they stay at our house for the weekend. We have a "family dinner" on Friday, and after the guests left this year, the fellows and I, with visits from Meagan and then Liv later, stayed up talking at the kitchen counter until 1 a.m., getting to know each other better.

The weekend was special. A thank-you note left on the counter read, "Thank you for welcoming us into your fellowship, city, hometown, home, family, and heart. Your words have changed me. I came to this place ready to start a job, but I'm leaving excited to step back, breathe, and enter three years of dramatic growth in professional development and emotional intelligence. Thank you for sharing your heart with us."

It's amazing, really. It turns out that what we want most in life is meaningful work and deep relationships, the chance to align our personal passion and professional mission. We relish the support we receive from like-minded souls and relax into our ability to support them equally. Near strangers who share a purpose and agree on a working methodology can become each other's people overnight. I've seen this year after year with the fellows.

Last summer I started writing a post called "The fellows are coming." I knew that writing about the experience of hosting the Rose Fellows at our house was an important part of the Tommy story, but for some reason I never wrote it. It was too raw, perhaps. When I entered the Rose Fellowship at age thirty-two, it had this same deep community-building impact on me. My life became a before-and-after story. It wasn't so much that I changed, but that the Fellowship was a chance for me to be my full self. Many of the Fellows have become my most trusted friends and closest touch points. Over the years, my relationship to the Fellowship has evolved, first as peer, then as mentor as the program director, but we are still primarily fellow travelers.

The Fellowship has also been in my girls' lives for the past seventeen years. Sophie was three and Liv was one when I started, and Bliss was born during my third year, going to her first construction site in the 10th and Page Street neighborhood at two and a half weeks old. The Fellowship has taken me to thirty-nine states and Puerto Rico, with eighty-five Fellows building more than 40,000 homes and making countless other contributions. The girls joined an epic trip to Puerto Rico with the Fellows, and they came to our cabin in Maine. Sophie came to Jamie and Drew's wedding in Santa Fe; Liv came to the anniversary retreat in Greenwood, Mississippi; Bliss came to Daniel and Rachel's wedding in Pennsylvania. Together we have gotten married, lost parents, had babies, lost a baby. We have gotten graduate degrees, changed jobs, run for office, moved across the country, moved to another country, and stayed put. Next week in San Ysidro I'll see David Flores, who has been working on behalf of his community on the border of Tijuana for seventeen years and counting. In Los Angeles I will see Theresa Hwang, who paved the way for Dawn in Venice. Our lives, our extended family, our people.

For the most part, I have brought my best self to this group. I know that relationships are what make the world go around, and that the quality of our relationships has a direct impact on the quality of our work. I have also failed. I can vividly remember moments of defensiveness, or saying the wrong thing, or not saying the right thing. I feel humbled by these wrong actions and non-actions. But mostly I feel proud that together we have created something larger than any individual—a perspective, a way of being, a commitment.

And so, "the fellows are coming" is part of who I am. Three years ago, when the Fellows came, Tommy and I had just met and I introduced him to my people. Two years ago we were newly engaged, and he knew how important these people were to me. He had traveled to New York to see their outgoing presentations and meet the crew. He met us in San Francisco and brought his sister to see us. Of course, he always ended up buying the drinks, footing the bill, making sure everyone had an extra slice of pizza at the end of the night. He did what he always did, which was to lean in, get to know, ask, learn, listen. So, by the time of our engagement, the Fellows evening was a full-on celebration.

Despite whatever professional and personal success I enjoyed, I had not had a true partner in my life for many years, and I was happy and proud. We drank champagne and toasted, and I basked in that moment with my beloved and my beloveds.

And so, when this new class came, they would be the first group to not meet Tommy. And yet, they enter this space with open hearts. They listen and relax into the Scarab, the symbol of rebirth and creativity, and one of them tells me, "He is here. We do know him. We know him through you." I wish that somehow I could model for them that one arrives somewhere certain in life. Adulthood. Success. You put in the work for a long time, but then you get there. You do get the experience and the maturity; you build your network; you deepen your perspective. You just don't always get it all the way you want it.

But there is always love. One of these fellows organized his introductory presentation around love. It is what drives us, connects us, and fuels this work. I am in good hands with these young people. They are wise and open. They are there for each other and they are there for me.

MARCH 11, 2018
Walled In by Kindness

"Everybody grieves differently." I hear this phrase all the time from well-meaning people who want to make space for people to express themselves, without pressure to act a certain way. But I wonder, is it true? There is so little discussion about grief that I cannot imagine how we would even know. Grief has become like a dark hole in my life; no one can see it. So maybe it's better to just say that everyone grieves differently, and leave it at that. There is no way to contest this statement.

I stopped by the Wellesley College archives today. The library must have by far the largest collection of Bates's work, and many are first editions. She donated her library to Wellesley, including rare books and letters. I found a book called *Round Robin* by Abbie Farwell Brown, president of the New England Poetry Society and children's book author. It is dedicated to "Katharine Lee Bates, Seer of Truth, Sayer of Beauty, Sower of Wisdom" and was signed by the author in 1921. There is untold treasure in this place.

In the archive are her diaries, unlike any I have ever seen. They are organized in a strange way, not linearly from one day to the next like a calendar, but rather organized by the number of the day: fifteen years of January 1sts on a single page. The first one spans from 1897 to 1911, the second from 1912 to 1926. I start with Bates's and Coman's birthdays (November 23 and August 12) and read first about happy days together: picnics in August, work in November. In the years after 1915, Coman's birthday is a dedicated day of memory.

And then I turn to January 11, scanning for the entry for that fateful day in 1915. It seems a miracle to be able to turn back the clock and read into Bates's mind. But I am not ready to read that yet. Instead, I turn to the first day of the year 1915.

> January 1: I stayed with the Old Year as long as I could, and when this dreaded New Year commenced after midnight, I could not welcome it.

I am struck by the very first entry and remember my New Year's entry: "*2017 will be the last year Tommy was alive. And that is a terrible thing to have in the past.*"

January 2: Katharine's "not feeling quite so strong" today . . .

January 3: Had the day with my blessed Katharine . . .

January 4: Busy in getting off my old MSS. Have found a new novel for Katharine . . .

January 5: . . . Never was there such a good department. Katharine stronger.

January 6: Extremely and unexpectedly difficult to take my seminar again, Olga returns. Katharine still stronger.

January 7: Katharine tries to do too much with Olga and is pathetically tired and restless.

January 8: All day Katharine has seemed to me very tired. With little break I began on "Booby."

January 9: Katharine had a "little pain in the left side." I spent the day close by her.

January 10: All night long my Darling was fighting for her breath. She was so weary today. I hardly left her.

I can hardly breathe. I want to read fast, to skim to the next entry, but Bates's handwriting is small and difficult to read, so I have to decipher as I go. I feel like I am reading a play; the tension has been mounting toward January 11. Some details are profound, others prosaic. Death is coming, I know it, but Bates does not, not yet. With Coman's four years of illness and many months confined to bed at the end, how was she to know the day? And I think of the morning of May 17, and my complete unknowing: "*I stayed in bed, captive audience to the coffee dance.*"

January 11: When I went in this morning at seven, Katharine raised her arms to me for help. I gave her what poor help I could until the end came quietly—Thank God for that!—at half-past nine.

Three lines on this fatal day, squeezed into two on the page. Twenty-five years together, two and a half hours at her side.

January 12: Strangely the days go by, the long, long hours. I think of my love "today" with Christ "in Paradise" this evening. *Strangely. Bates's first day-after word is "strangely."*

I read on, rapt.

January 13: A violent storm postpones . . . But we had the home service as we had planned. Very beautifully she keeps her quiet state in Bohemia. *"I feel his beautiful, still self, somehow peaceful despite my mounting anguish."*

January 14: The weather cleared and we went to Mount Auburn where the beautiful mortal put on immortality. *"We stood and watched as he was honored, the flag him, he the flag, as he was folded once, twice, again and again, so neatly, so squarely, into a perfect recognizable package, and handed, complete, to his son."*

January 15: Seymour Coman left this morning to bear his strange burden to the family resting place in Newark. *"I wish he were here to voice his opinion."*

January 16: Dr. Raymond helps me in bed today. *"Meagan brings the baby. Lisa rubs my back."*

January 17: It is hard to be valiant, to be brave where one is half ill, but Katharine was valiant to the last. *"This is what we practice for."*

January 18: I don't know why this heart of mine should go on beating when Katharine's heart is ashes, but it does.

Reading becomes nearly impossible. I cannot cry and let tears drop on these precious diaries. I look over at the archivist, the quiet total in this serious room, the rules enforced. But it's overwhelming, as if my life has been captured in a sentence, fragments really, brief but to the point. The poet, the poet: "I don't know why this heart of mine should go on beating when Katharine's heart is ashes, but it does." How does a soul write this one week after the love of her life has died? How can such beauty and such pain coexist? I think back, again and again, to these words, rushing through me, shaping my emotions the way water shapes rocks: *"This vertiginous feeling of falling in love, now more than ever, of not being able to separate his soul from mine, of his spirit leaving his body as I held it in my hands."*

January 19: Dr. Raymond's wonderful red roses have helped, and with this sunset come beautiful pink roses from Mr. Coman. *"Last week's flowers died, and new ones arrive."*

January 20: Am trying to work, but even a note seems a big effort. Olga and Jean both show reactions from the strain. *"Now with him gone, I feel those rough edges."*

January 21: Jean was ill last night but better today. We had Miss Hunt for dinner but I found entertaining a strain. More roses from S. C. *"At least this summer, this week, this month, this year, we get to speak about him."*

January 22: I live with Katharine in spirit and sometimes as tonight, can almost feel her smiling in my soul. *"I see you as intertwined vines."*

January 23: . . . I pored over her letters, but she must have been busy in some far part of heaven for I could not find her . . . *"You can't call that a dream, then, if you weren't really sleeping."*

January 24: I spent the day over the resume of Katharine's illness, such a long, heroic, fruitful martyrdom. *"My curiosity only grew, my admiration intensified."*

January 25: I have a little paradise of my own, all walled in by kindness, a rose garden where I live with Katharine's spirit. *"You cannot unsee the kindness of others."*

January 26: Wrote this morning, but with difficulty . . . More red roses from S. C. *"Writing and grieving seemed the same to me."*

January 27: Still writing my Beloved's illness. Mrs. Day came for letters this afternoon. *"Writing is my happiest time now."*

January 28: Writing this morning. Mrs. Day more letters. This afternoon S. C.'s roses— pink, white, red . . . *"Every day, the mailbox is full of handwritten notes."*

January 29: Still shut into my Paradise of roses with Katharine but the summons to work begins to knock at the door. *"There is pleasure in action, pleasure in production."*

January 30: A wreath of flowers again . . . *"The flowers, cards, lunches, and cut strawberries."*

January 31: The memorial service tonight was beautiful and triumphant, but it was harder for me to bear than I had foreseen. *"There was no one in the church who hadn't cried during the service, not one who could accept the unfairness of this loss."*

It's enough. Bates seemed to live a year of my processes in two weeks. Bearing the unbearable grief, the care and kindness, the paradise of roses, the kindness, the need to write, the summons to work.

Sitting in the archive only a half mile from home, imagining the path that the Katies walked daily, tramping through the woods between the Scarab and the campus they loved so dearly. Imagining the view from Bohemia to this very spot, the two of them watching the fire on the early morning of May 17, 1914, that engulfed The Tower, which had been the heart of the Wellesley community since it was built in 1875, the year before the young Ms. Bates began. I can see the Katies watching the smoke from the third floor of Bohemia, Coman no doubt in bed, likely never again to step foot on campus, watching, a perfect view of their beloved, burning community, almost like they could be looking over me now, deep in the library on their campus.

But my viewshed expands, to not just include space, but time, holding us in the space of the pure experience of humanness. A hundred years folds into a few lines scratched out in a journal, the raw realness of now, still present. Maybe we do all grieve the same way—not at the same speed or in the same order, but maybe we are more alike than we are different. Maybe it is in moments of profound loss (or love!) that we are the most alike. At that moment of loss, instead of being isolated, we can connect, over time and through space, to some essential fact. We can bring death and the experience of grief into our present, into our world, and share in this experience together.

APRIL 22, 2018
Shavasana, Again

It is the first real weekend of spring, gorgeous weather, cool but sunny with bright-blue skies and the bright-blue water of Long Island Sound. I spend a long weekend at my friend Jennie's house in Quogue with Debbie and Sue Ann and our girls. We take a long walk on the beach, maybe an hour in each direction. Tommy is everywhere in the change in light and season; this is his time of year—the beach and the sand and the round stones, and the shocking cold of the spring ocean. I feel myself shifting again, and while the tears had been fairly well bottled up recently, now they flow easily, like spring has reopened those channels.

Debbie and Sue Ann are getting cold and a little impatient to leave, but they make room for me; there's nowhere we need to be. The girls are out for a run and have planned a shopping day ahead. I need to pause. I put up the hood of my vest and lie down on my back in the sand. Shavasana is where I find him most completely. Except that today I'm not imagining the sound of waves, the feeling of sun on my face, the sand giving way beneath me; I'm physically here. I settle in.

Shavasana was always a time Tommy and I were together, but now it's different. I feel his body growing still and imagine that as mine grows still under the blue sky, I get closer to him, as if he is waiting for me. I am on the coast of New Zealand; I am on Nantucket; I am on the swimming dock, floating. It is his birthday, and while we've known him only a little more than two months, he is wholly ours and we are his. How did the girls know so quickly and completely? I don't know, but I've learned to trust that.

I am glad he was cremated. I can't stand the thought of his body decaying. I'm grateful that he could go from his dynamic, living self to total stillness. The ashes are still sitting on a shelf at the funeral home, and May 17 is coming. I feel some panic; shouldn't they be spread? No matter, Katie, no matter; breathe in the sea air and feel the sun on your face; it's okay. I have to trust in his patience, his calm, his long view. Stay in the knowledge that the most important part of him, his spirit and his soul, are just where they need to be, alive and moving within me, within us.

MAY 13, 2018
Mother's Day (2)

"We are one," you told me so many times. I can't remember the first time you said it, but it defined us from the beginning. I still see the faint outline of "there is an us" written in the dust of my windshield that first Easter morning. I still feel how profoundly you shifted the chemistry of me to us, how completely one I feel with you. After you were first gone, I found myself thinking, "What would Tommy do?" or "What would Tommy say?" It became a touch point. What you would do or say was always the highest embodiment of me. But over time I've noticed that I have to ask that less. There are moments when I get afraid and anxious, but mostly now I am okay. I just know. I am us, you are me, we are one.

But what I miss so desperately is being two. I miss your hand holding mine. I miss the feel of your body near me, leading, following, alongside. The girls beat Westwood yesterday, first time in Wellesley girls' lacrosse history. It was the first time in as long as anyone can remember. Did you hear? Did you see? I had to watch from the field, though, because I could not bring myself to walk up those bleacher steps without you—you taking two steps at a time, powerful thighs and easy grace, holding my hand. The pleasure of sitting next to you, feeling your shoulder and knee touching mine.

I miss our three too—you and Bliss and me. She is so sad. I cannot make up for the loss of you two—so well did you complete each other, so much did you fuel and inspire her, so much did you bask in each other's love.

I miss the foursome of double dates, the sense that we were a pair ready for matching. I miss our five, the girls and you and me and the home we created together. I miss our six, seven, and eight. I miss the boys. I am trying, trying to be one, four, seven. It's harder without you, my perfect one.

The card says "One Perfect Day" on the cover, and there is a string of butterflies. It is Mother's Day, May 8, 2016. Tommy writes in his beautiful handwriting:

Dear Katie,

It has been a blessing to witness an amazing woman and mother raise three extraordinary young women! Your house is so much more than a home, and what you have already shared, taught and given to them will carry them, happily and confidently through their lives.

Your lives together as a family are indescribably beautiful . . . In a parallel universe, you are with me and my boys and we were are one, as it shall be . . .

With all my love and adoration,

Tommy

MAY 15, 2018
Joy of Life

The mystery of the elevator is solved. When I first bought the Scarab, there was a small, rectangular hole in each floor. What could it possibly have been used for? A newspaper article quotes the son of the architect remembering that his father had installed an elevator for Bates, intimating that her weight made it hard for her to use the stairs. Many accounts of Bates describe her as pudgy; the picture many writers painted was that her lively spirit was somehow betrayed by her ungainly body. But was it? She walked and rode her bike to campus every day she taught. She traveled the world, climbed mountains, sailed across the sea and down the Nile River. Coman was portrayed as the more athletic of the two, lean, spritely. But of course, Coman got sick and died at age fifty-seven, while Bates died at age seventy. We have learned that the timing of death is unpredictable.

The elevator, it turns out, was not for Bates at all, but rather Bates had it installed for Coman. From 1911, when Coman was diagnosed, until her death in January 1915, Coman still managed to travel quite a bit: a trip to England and France one summer, a visit home to Michigan, trips to friends' houses nearby. But ultimately she retreated to Bohemia. During those four years, she worked on a reissue of *The Industrial History of the United States* and *The Industrial History of New England* (unpublished).

Bates installed the elevator so Coman could come downstairs for dinner and to meet guests. I love this act of love and how it manifested itself in the architecture. Now I can see them more clearly, these beloveds. I wish we had left the trace in the floorboards of Bohemia, but the hole is still there in the subfloor under the new pine boards.

Bates's letter to Coman's friends and family turns out to be the first first-hand account of breast cancer. These were remarkable women, the force of their persons propelling them into history even in this most intimate space. They were known for their scholarship and teaching—Bates for her poetry and cultivation of poets, Coman for her groundbreaking perspective on economics, believing that economics must be seen in the context of history and the lives of real people, especially women, the poor, and immigrants.

Coman was part of the Settlement House movement, started a local pre-school, and got involved in labor strikes. Bates was a member of the New England Poetry Society and for years hosted poets at the Scarab, encouraging their careers. Teaching and scholarship had always united and guided them, and they collaborated directly on *From Gretna Green to Land's End: A Literary Journal in England*, with text by Bates and photographs by Coman. Their scholarship and place in academic history is solid, but their story contributed so much more. Many look to them as early pioneers of female love, in a so-called Boston Marriage, an unknown concept at the time when all female sexuality was seen only though the male lens. But for me, it is the quality of their love that is the most compelling.

They were partners in the modern sense. Intimate, domestic, social, and professional partners; cheerleader and amplifier. They traveled alone and together, taking pleasure both in each other's presence and describing their journey to each other, sharing in letters and no doubt conversation about where they had been, what they had seen and learned. They had different causes, but they were united in their support for the other.

MAY 20, 2018
The Sky-Parlor

I had been meaning to get to Concord for a while. It's the historic center of New England, and my sister and I used to take the kids to Louisa May Alcott's Orchard House and to the Concord Museum when they were young. I was pregnant with Bliss at the time, and we had taken Sophie, Liv, and my niece and nephew, Phoebe and Charlie, to see the storybook-themed Christmas trees. I saw the name Phebe Bliss Emerson (1741–1829), and while the idea for Bliss's name originated from a beloved nursery school teacher in Charlottesville, that day confirmed the decision: Bliss would be called Bliss, unlikely as it seemed then, perfect as it is now.

In Concord today for lacrosse, I have a couple of hours before taking Bliss and her friends home; it's my perfect window. First stop is to the home of Ralph Waldo Emerson, his residence of forty-seven years (1835–1882), and for his second wife, Lidian Jackson Emerson, another ten after his death. His children had the foresight to keep the home, and now it is a museum, preserved as it was in his day. I am there to learn about Hawthorne, who I knew had rented a home from Emerson, but I have to start at the beginning, with Emerson himself.

The tour guides relay that Emerson's life was defined by love . . . and grief. He met and fell deeply in love with his first wife, Ellen Louisa Tucker Emerson. Beautiful and well read, with a dog named Yeats, Ellen was only sixteen when they met but already suffering from tuberculosis. They were engaged and married; she was to be a poet and he a minister.

They had been utterly in love, and for a moment, on September 30, 1829, their wedding day, the future had seemed clear. Notes and letters flew back and forth. They traveled and wrote verses together and laughed at the Shakers who had tried to woo them to celibacy. The book *Emerson: The Mind on Fire* starts at Ellen's gravesite, with Emerson consumed with grief and doubt, opening her casket at a cemetery in Roxbury fourteen months after her death. (What was he doing?) Her death filled him with a grief that threw everything he knew into question. His brother Charles wrote, "Waldo is sick . . . I never saw him so disheartened . . . things seem to be flying to pieces." Love. Loss. Grief. Life coming unhinged, the impossibility of things being the same as before. Grief led to doubt of the church and Emerson's conversion to transcendentalism; he gave up his career in the church and chose writing and speaking.

"Is there a third floor in this house?" I ask, looking for Hawthorne in this place. No, the tour guide says, just an attic. But after some discussion, she says, "Oh, you must be thinking of Wayside, next to Orchard House." I had passed the Alcott house earlier that day, with people dressed in historical costumes out in the yard, staging a reenactment. The girls and I, fans of *Little Women*, had been there many times. I had never heard of Wayside.

As I head just a half mile down the street, this jumble of a house comes into view. It started as an old-fashioned saltbox and was added to so many times: a rounded screened-in porch, multiple additions. But there, looming, oddly, in the rear, is a kind of tower. A third-story room, sitting at the top of this house. I never once imagined there was a literal precedent for

Bohemia, but here it is! This creative writing space, this room above the domestic, a tree house.

I also hadn't realized that Nathaniel Hawthorne's wife, Sophia Peabody, was such a force of her own: an artist, a painter, a prodigious creative. Sophia and Nathaniel were engaged for three years, I learn at the bookstore in the Old Manse, before they were married, trying to sort out how to keep their creative lives intact while joining as a couple. In the early days of their courtship, Sophia made an illustration for "The Gentle Boy," a story in Hawthorne's *Twice-Told Tales*. Once the children came, however, the gender roles asserted themselves, and Sophia took on the childrearing as Nathaniel continued to write.

I knew from Alice Friedman that the Katies had the Hawthornes in mind when they envisioned the ideal of a creative partnership, grounded in both love and work, reflected in their daily schedules, and their architecture. Coman contributed the photography for Bates's books, and Bohemia may have held a darkroom as well as being the creative writing space high above the domestic realm.

But this tree house is too much. I am in awe of this ungainly structure, the effort and imagination required. It looks completely out of place here in Concord. "Hawthorne . . . returned to the Wayside, where he would build himself a third-story tower, twenty feet square, a sky-parlor he called it, modeled roughly on the tower of the Villa Montauto. There, he'd write high above the fray, entering his sanctum through a trap door, he told Longfellow, on which he'd plant his chair."

Ah, it all comes into focus, as if this last piece of the puzzle has finally fit. The architectural mystery signals a key to relationships built on the idea of partnerships that navigate the creative production of each partner while also accommodating work and life within the domestic sphere. The architecture of what we now call "live-work" representing something far greater: the activation of love as a source of creativity.

Bohemia holds a special place in this trajectory. The third-floor sky-parlor may have been its inspiration; but Bohemia was fully integrated into the original design of the house, not an addition. These women built an architecture that allows for the fullest expression of their creative selves, at home but also above the daily rituals. No wonder. No wonder we found our home here, this place that allowed us to be fully in love with each other and at peace with ourselves, productive and still, lively and restful, expansive and whole.

MAY 23, 2018

His Way Is Now Our Way

We made it, I suppose. The one-year anniversary, May 17, has passed. We had dreaded its arrival. Bliss declared that she wanted to stay in bed and eat candy all day. Liv said she wouldn't predict what she wanted to do. Sophie was at school; my friend Heather gave her son Carter money to take her out to dinner that night. But as the day got closer, we got more intentional. We were transitioning. We were not the family in the darkest moment of grief now; we were the family one year later. During that year, Sophie's best friend's mother died suddenly. Sophie rushed back from school (again) to be there, to write the obituary, to help plan the funeral, knowing how to do this.

Would I reverse the course of history? Yes. Would I have him back for anything? Yes. But what a gift it is to see your children mature before your eyes, to become radically empathetic, to understand death and love and life, to be able to give that gift to others.

"What about going to Nantucket?" I lobby, ready for the girls to say no. Yes, they say, lighting up. I cannot believe it. I go up to Bohemia immediately to book a hotel, reserve the ferry. We will go for just one overnight, leaving Thursday and coming home Friday, to spend the day in one of Tommy's favorite places on earth.

But first, we call our friends. By Wednesday at 8 p.m. the house is pulsing. The freshmen in the basement, the seniors in the kitchen, the grownups in the living room, music spilling, lights on, driveway packed with cars. "Come over for a hug" was the invitation, and our community shows up with little or no advance notice. They want it too, of course.

By the time we get out to the beach on Friday, the wind is wild and the ocean surges. In Nantucket, Bliss can put her head in my lap, Liv can stroll down Main Street with me arm in arm, the artifice of home slips away, and intimacy can reassert itself. I had already told Bliss about the metaphor my therapist shared with me earlier in the week:

In life, you are the surfer. Your job is to stay on the board and surf. The waves will come and go, some big, some small, some powerful, some boring. Some will take you down; others you will ride in ecstasy. You are not the wave. You are the surfer. The only thing you know about the wave is that another will come, the size and shape of which you have no idea. As the surfer, your job is to ride the wave. Stay on your board. Or if you fall off, get back on.

I pause and say, "I'm not really sure what the board is." The girls step in, "The surfboard is your family, your community." It is what keeps you safe, keeps you afloat.

And in this moment, I know for sure that we have done it. I also know that we will have to keep doing it, again and again. I am overwhelmed by the beauty and fierceness of these children, this life, this moment. Tommy has changed us forever by opening degrees of sadness we never knew existed, but also degrees of love we could never have dreamed of. He is with us, and we are okay. His way is now our way.

We get to keep the gifts he gave us.

Afterword

It will be three years "after" by the time these words are published. Life for us has continued. Life for Tommy, shockingly still, has not. Year two, year three . . . these are questions too big to be addressed in this tiny afterword. But this writing from year one has been written indelibly into me. It feels as if the act of writing created pathways for my recovery. I think of it like skiing in fresh powder or hiking an unknown trail. The first time you do it, it's hard. But once you have carved the path, it gets easier. Fear, self-pity, and crippling sadness are always there, lurking. But when I feel a wave of self-pity coming, I can usually get myself onto the path of gratitude. When I feel sadness taking over, I know that love is its antidote. I have done it before; I can do it again. So many people have made this path navigable for me from their experience and wisdom, and I hope that my experience will in turn make it easier for others.

There is a lot I left out. A friend recently wrote, "I smiled when I read 'the fucking pachysandra.' Until this point, Tommy had seemed like a saint among men—almost too pure to be real." Was he perfect, were we perfect? Here I get into a bit of trouble because in my mind, the answer is yes. We aren't in any way perfect people, but together we were perfect. I feel like the challenges we faced were external to us, and so they didn't enter my grief narrative. I wrote to talk with him, understand him, be with him, and conflict was not a part of that. Maybe as our relationship matured, we would have had more disagreements, but strangely, I can't remember any of substance. Actually, I remember one big fight we had! I won't share all the details, but suffice it to say that we had made an agreement about how to handle a conflict, and while I was in San Francisco on business, he broke our pact and the situation flared up. I got home on Friday night, late, still mad. He didn't live with us yet; it was the first winter of our relationship. The girls were gone and I came home to a dark, empty house. I was in the middle of painting the front hall, and I changed into painting clothes and started, burning off my anger. Tommy came by in his business clothes. He stripped to his boxers and painted with me. We painted and talked (madly at first, calmly later) for hours, finally just being done with both the hall and the fight. One of his friends later told me that Tommy had told him the story and said that the best part about us was that we fought naked. Ha!

The stories I tell about Tommy's life are the ones I know, from his tellings and retellings, from my own limited time with him, and the ones that sprang onto my keyboard. There is so much more to his life that was not mine to know or tell. But I cherish every memory, every story, every detail from my time with this remarkable man. This is my story. I have thought of it as a love-and-grief story, but mostly it is a love story. A love letter to my beloved.

Your sentence by my quavering voice was told,
I Give you joy, my Dearest. Death is done.

Obituary: Thomas Edward Niles

Thomas Edward Niles of Wellesley, MA, formerly of Needham, MA, passed away unexpectedly on May 17th. Tommy is survived by his sons Aaron, Benjamin and Caleb of Needham and their mother Susan; his fiancée Katie Swenson and her daughters Sophie, Olivia and Bliss of Wellesley; his four older siblings, Peter Niles (Nancy), Marguerite Grieco (Brien), Connie Alford (Kevin), Mary Jane Niles (John Higgins); and his nieces and nephews Adrienne Kinkade, Alex Grieco, Daniel Millen, and Connor Alford. He is preceded in death by his parents, Mary Jane Furey Niles and Glenn Harding Niles.

Tommy was born on May 25, 1960 in Elmira, New York, the youngest of five children. He attended Elmira Free Academy High School, where he excelled in football, baseball and basketball. As a senior, he was named Class Athlete and received the Ernie Davis Award, which was especially meaningful because Davis, also a graduate of Elmira Free Academy and the first African-American to win the Heisman Trophy, was an idol for Tommy. Football was his passion. He was awarded a scholarship to the University of Rhode Island, where he received the Scholar Athlete Award. His love for the game provided him with a family of friends who remained dear to him throughout his life. Known for his sharp intellect and far-reaching love of history, science, math and philosophy, he graduated in 1984 with a degree in civil engineering and was awarded Tau Beta Pi honors from the National Engineering Honors Society.

While at URI, Tommy completed ROTC and was commissioned in the United States Army in 1983 as a 2nd lieutenant. He served as a Company Commander in the Army National Guard and was awarded the Meritorious Service Medal and Army Commendation Medal. He served as a troop commander in Italy and Croatia. While in the service, Tommy relished in the opportunity to travel Europe, particularly in and around Venice. He retired from the service in 1991 as a Captain.

Tommy married Susan Hylka and moved to Needham where he raised his beloved sons, Aaron, Ben and Caleb. He coached his sons and many

Needham boys in Pop Warner Football, Little League Baseball, and even hockey, despite not having played the game himself. He built rinks in his backyard and hosted many beautiful days of skating, sometimes with music or a movie projector. In college, he was a lifeguard for the Town of Nantucket and later realized his dream of building a home there, where his children enjoyed many magical summers. He had enormous love for each of his sons and treasured being their father.

Tommy started his career in real estate and development in Providence in 1983, building transformative urban projects across the country. He joined Trammell Crow Company in Boston in 1989. As a Principal, he was responsible for developing commercial, hotel and retail assets, including the award-winning conversion and rehabilitation of the Batterymarch Hilton Hotel, a historic 1929 Art-Deco tower. Tommy joined NeXcomm Capital Partners in 2000, where he was responsible for real estate acquisitions and development. In 2002, he founded NPV Development where his projects included Waterplace Park in Providence. In 2004, he partnered with CV Properties to develop American Brewery Lofts, a 79-unit historic restoration in Boston. As Sr. Vice President and Principal at CV Properties, he continued to oversee numerous developments, many of them renovations of cherished historic properties, including the Art-deco rehabilitation project redevelopment of Post Office Square Tower. In 2016, he opened the Aloft and Element Hotels in Boston's Seaport District with much acclaim. He was leading the development of South Street Landing in Providence, RI, the historic rehabilitation of a century-old power plant, which will welcome Brown University and the RI Nursing Education Center in the Fall of 2017.

Tommy was also deeply committed to making a tangible difference in the lives of others. He was especially devoted to the South Shore YMCA and was named to the Chairman's Roundtable in recognition for his visionary stewardship of the design and completion of an innovative new building which nurtures the rich diversity and inclusive spirit of the Quincy community.

On March 11, 2015, he met Katie Swenson and began a rich and loving new chapter in his life. He later told Katie that this day "led to many of the happiest days of my life." Grounded in unwavering love and support for each other and their shared commitment to their six children, they experienced a love that touched and inspired the many people in their lives. Tommy embraced Katie's daughters as his own, and they in turn opened their hearts to his infectious smile and irresistible kindness. Tommy was engaged to Katie, the love of his life, on April 4, 2016 and they were to be married on July 22, 2017.

Despite his excellent health, Tommy suffered a heart attack on the early morning of May 17th. Katie and his cherished sons were by his side.

Everyone who knew Tommy was blessed to be his friend. Everyone was touched by his grace and love. He was a gentle soul who made you feel welcome and at ease. He was kind and principled, and he had a curiosity and delight for the world around him. Most of all, he cherished and was incredibly proud of all of his children. He will be deeply missed.

Home of
KATHERINE LEE BATES,
author of
"America the Beautiful"
1907 - 1929

Wellesley Historical Society

The Scarab, home of Katharine Lee Bates

Top: the Scarab, circa 1950–1955; *bottom*: the Scarab, 2019

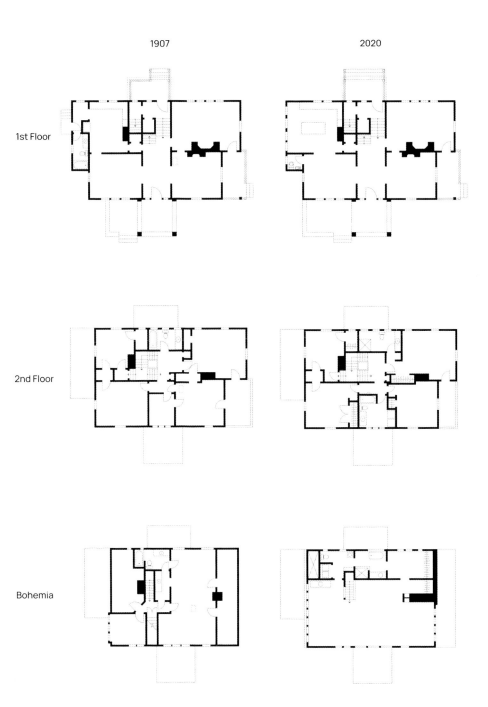

1907   2020

1st Floor

2nd Floor

Bohemia

Plans of the Scarab, re-created from 1907 plan and 2020 plan

Top and bottom: Bohemia, 2019

Katie Swenson and Tommy Niles, 2016

Katharine Coman at Wellesley College, 1885

Katharine Lee Bates at the Scarab, circa 1916

"There is a faith in me that tells me I shall not forget my lover though God forget the world." + Katharine (1915)
— Fletcher's *Hassan* + Mrs. Scudder (1920)

JANUARY 11

Thur 1912	Nor very fine. Zero weather. But I have a good time with the four newly-discovered plays of Menander.
Sat 1913	Poor little Chito died this morning, and the Doctor's voice broke at the telephone. She did not come alive.
SUN 1914	The event of today was the distribution of gifts by the Cardinal to the poor children. Katharine and I discussed the coming years.
Mon 1915	When I went in this morning at seven, Katharine raised her arms to me for help. I gave her what poor help I could till the end came quietly — thank God for that! — at half past nine.
Tues 1916	Emily, Marion, Dr. Raymond send flowers for the precious memory. Olga, too, and Miss Marsh and Cousin Sarah. Emily comes
Thur 1917	Marion, Dr. Raymond, Cousin Sarah, Olga, all send flowers and Vida telephones. I resume college work.
Fri 1918	Only a little time with Katharine in Bohemia. Mamie came to luncheon. Then there was Department.
Sat 1919	Katharine's day. I was busy at College from nine till four, but Miss Sarah came this evening, bringing Easter lilies.
SUN 1920	Katharine seemed to lean over my bed this morning, with the one brave word; "Unselfishness." Mrs. Scudder's soul passed almost at Katharine's very hour.
Tues 1921	Wrote another of the Corona III sonnets. Marion came to see me and Olga took me up to hear Tagore this evening.
Wed 1922	Went to Philadelphia, where Mame lay among her flowers, and Will and Marie and a blessed baby welcomed me.
Thur 1923	Went into town, had some help from Dr. Allen, saw something of William and Kennet and came home this' the snow very tired.
Fri 1924	I wanted the day to be in Heaven and it opened with domestic trouble over a bread-mixer. Marion came. Vida remembered.
SUN 1925	Again Marion and Vida remembered. I had the morning in dear Bohemia. Levalards and Brainerds called this afternoon.
Mon 1926	Marion and Vida and Miss Blaisdell remembered, sending heather and pink roses and calendulas. Peace and joy are surely here.

Page from the journals of Katharine Lee Bates

In Bohemia: A Corona of Sonnets

BY KATHARINE LEE BATES

(I)

I give you joy, my Dearest. Death is done,
Your martyrdom accomplished, and your crown
Of sainthood, woven of such pains as drown
Remembering eyes in tears, superbly won.
No stain upon your faith's white splendor, none;
No moment when you cast your courage down,
A broken sword. You enter with renown
Out of these shadows into radiant sun.
Gone, gone; yet still we pore upon your face.
Your face already strange in sculptured pallor.
Listening, but not to us; your face, a scroll
Frailer than parchment, where we yet may trace
A holy script. O loyalty! O valor!
Your voice still echoes: "Bless the Lord, my soul."

Your voice still echoes: "Bless the Lord, my soul,
And all that is within me, bless His name!"
All, all within you? The disease, the shame
Let loose in your pure body sweet and whole
Beyond the wont of flesh, till evil stole
On those unconscious tissues, torment came
As furtively as some slow-creeping flame
Corroding from within the golden bowl?
Yea, verily, your body's bitter woe
In your divine endurance blessed the Lord.
Your youth of bounding pulses, one clear choir
Of joy and strength and glorious desire,
Could lift no strain of adoration so
Poignant, angelic, suffering's master-chord.

Poignant, angelic, suffering's master-chord,
Your music rings through my bewildered days,
A worship, and my spirit strives to raise
Thanksgiving with your own, above this horde
Of griefs, rebellions, yearnings. Oh, afford
From your rich joy, in your old, generous ways,
Largess to me, that my torn heart may praise
Death, even Death, your healing, your reward.
Death entered, bearer of the only key
That could unlock the iron gates of pain.
The Angel of the Lord, our very love
Knelt in his shining, as he smote the chain
From off your limbs, and swift you rose, set free.
Forever free. My heart, be glad thereof!

It was heart's woe, Most Beautiful my Friend,
To watch your bright hair wither, shoulders bend
Beneath the burden. White as carrier-dove
Your numb, forgetful hand, an empty glove,
Lies on a quiet breast the hard gasps rend
No longer. From the broken cage ascend,
God's homing bird, to boundless air above.
Your joy shall be my joy,—ay, though the word
Chokes to a sob. My tragedy is done.
I could laugh upon the stroke even of Orion's
Great, gleaming sword, dull by comparison
With that keen pang unbearable that heard
Your only moan: "My soul is among lions."

Your only moan: "My soul is among lions."
You were on shipboard, sailing home to die.
I sat beside you on the deck; the sky
Glistened with constellations, starry scions
Of an eternal fire. Not white-hot irons

Could so have seared my spirit as that cry
From your deep anguish. You will know me by
That scar through joys of all imagined Zions.
You, you, so light to leap, so fleet to race.
Eager for burdens, I must see you shorn
Of all those ardors, slowly dispossessed
Of your proud heritage, turning your face
Toward Death, your face each dawn more wan, more worn.
I could not make him an unwelcome guest.

I could not make him an unwelcome guest,
For that dim morning, when I raised the shade
Upon the joy of sunrise, you essayed
To look with eyes that pleaded but for rest,
So weary, O so weary. Peace was best.
Yet as Death hushed the breath, your love delayed
His touch an instant, while your white lips made
Effort to smile on me, a last behest
Of courage. Ah, such little time before
In panting torture you had lifted arms
To me for help I could not, could not give;
Yet in your utmost weakness, you restore
My fainting strength. Delivered from all harms
In your deliverance. Dear Heart, I live.

In your deliverance. Dear Heart, I live.
The olive cross you loved for Bethlehem,
Slipt under your chill hand, with lily-stem,
Merges in your mortality. We give
Your tired beauty, wistful, fugitive.
To chariot of fire. Your requiem
Is chanted. Prayer and holy apothegm
Are uttered. All is ashes, where no sieve
Shall find forever form or face of you.

But in your upper chamber, in your own
Bohemia, wide-windowed to the sun,
We are together, all our suffering through.
Our long suspense and dread a shadow flown.
I give you joy, my Dearest. Death is done.

(II)

Our word shall still be Joy, shall still be Joy.
Death shall not be a frost that blackens all
The blossoms in our garden. Love, I call
To mind your life on earth, so to employ
My aching thoughts, lest lurking grief decoy
My spirit from its vow. And yet they fall.
Slow tears, on even this cramped, childish scrawl
Of hidden verses that you bade destroy.
Where is that child, with wide gray eyes of wonder
And broad braids yellow as the prairie moon
Whereon she gazed, suggesting with sage thrift
To cut it into stars would be a boon,
'Twould make so many? Ah, sweet childhoods, plunder
Of Time's fast wings, an April petal-drift!

From Time's fast wings, an April petal-drift
These songs have fluttered back, secretly penned,
A murmurous joy, deep in the leafy bend
Of silver-maple or in fragrant rift
Of haystack. Were these ten small leaves a gift
From Father's desk, this desk become my friend
As it was his and yours? Did Mother mend
With magic thread these rough-torn pages whiffed
Down half a century that changed the child
From form to form, a maid for men's desire.
Scholar with quarreling books about her piled,
Far traveller, sufferer, ashes on the pyre?

How fierce an anguish to the spirit brings
This mocking immortality of things!

The mocking immortality of things
Shall be forgiven to this tiny tome
For its dear childishness,—epic of home,
Ohio farm with joy of watersprings
And cedars full of crystal carollings;
Slow cows to drive and cosset lambs to comb;
Sheep deftly yoked to turn the garden loam
For labor-saving brothers; venturings
Of emulous fleets that sailed the orchard brook,
The proudest topped by mousetrap cabin where
A frog sat skipper with a pompous look.
Such hours are of their beauty unaware,
White daisies dancing in a meadow nook,
Till wistful memory beholds them fair.

Your wistful memory beheld them fair
And still more fair as further they receded,
Those childhood scenes dawn-colored and dew-beaded.
All needments but few luxuries were there
In that true home,—joyance of sun-steeped air,
Tasks bubbling into frolic, hearts that heeded
High voices, eager summer days that speeded
To tranquil twilights. Grouped about the chair
Where Mother with her mending took such rest
As mothers may, on doorsteps fronting west
Father and lads and lassies watched the strange
Drama of sunset, glimpsing crown and wing
And many a cloudy shape swift vanishing
By nature's mandate of eternal change.

By nature's mandate of eternal change
That group has melted, like those shifting gleams
Of air, a vision, one of many dreams
That haunt the levels of that lonely grange.
The soldier father was the first to range
Beyond the sunset, he whom war's extremes
Had wellnigh shattered, who from battle themes
Turned sharply, as from thoughts he would estrange.
The children's games of war he could not brook.
Their Shiloh with small fallen heroes woke
So deep a horror in his brooding look
They ceased to play at slaughter, yet no less
Joyed to behold him honored of the folk
For manhood, as his wife for graciousness.

Hers, when I knew her, was the graciousness
Of one long regnant on the quiet throne
Of love,—such love as tender children own
For parents whom the heavy years oppress;
Such love as she in turn poured back to bless
Their varying ways with steadfast music, known
From cradle-time as life's sweet undertone,
The mother-love, unfailing, measureless.
And forth from love there blossomed such high graces,
Courage and courtesy, joy, wisdom clear.
A fortitude forbidding all complaints,
That while she walketh now in heavenly places,
I think the very stars must hold her dear
And do her reverence as a queen of saints.

You did her reverence as a queen of saints
Many glad years together. When she passed
Beyond your touch, your faith still held her fast,
And as our human longing ever paints

Its Paradise with flush of earth, and faints
Before sheer spirit, so in that dread vast
You saw her waiting, loving arms outcast,
In the old happy doorway. What constraints
Were those that led your brother's questing feet
To even such homestead on a Berkshire hill
For your last summer? Winds across the wheat.
Frolic of calves, familiar farm employ
Closed up your circle, while our word was still
—O breaking hearts!—while still our word was Joy.

(III)

I could not bear my grief but that I must.
Is it not you who live, while I am dead,
Cold as that stone whereon the fire was red,
Now left alone to lichen or to dust?
"Thoughts of a Stone" your title has it, just
A bit of baby lyric, yet you said
What here I prove,—the campfire glows are spread
And trampled, picnic over, not a crust
Of joy dropt for the stone whence flames rose bright,
So bright it deemed itself a thing of fire.
And I must bear this grief night after night.
Day after day, through weeks and months and years,
This grief become myself, too dull for tears,
Bewildered past all pain, past all desire.

Bewildered past all pain, past all desire,
I stare forever on a snowy scene,
Blue glint of crusted drifts, the irised green
Of frost-filmed pines, impertinence of spire
And joy-lit panes, till shoot of anguish, dire
As crematory heats within whose keen
Embraces dies your beauty that has been,

Stings me to consciousness. Then I inquire
Of my forgotten senses, and I learn,
Noting accustomed walls and voices near,
I am no longer tranced in that return
From white Mount Auburn, where we left you, Dear,
—No, no, not you; a worn-out robe to burn,
Even as this globe shall gleam and disappear.

Even as this globe shall gleam and disappear,
My life has vanished, life of joy I led
Folded in yours. Never again to tread
The station platform, tired scrutineer
Of every face, until a sudden cheer
Tingles through all my veins, fatigue is sped,
For you are with me, sweet as daily bread,
Refreshing as cool water! Oh, the mere
Touch of your hand, your hand that now is ashes,
Turned all the day's vexations into mirth.
Beside you in the car, its groaning pull
And grinding brakes and harsh metallic crashes
Made blither music than remains on earth;
And yet I wonder I am sorrowful.

I wonder I am sorrowful, for now
There is no pain to fear for you. The sting
Of death is drawn. Escaped from suffering,
The crown of thorns is lifted from your brow.
I wonder I am sorrowful, for how
Can I be warped with winter, when the spring
Floods your free spirit, and its raptures wing
Your golden flight from our bare mortal bough?
Yet, Ever Dearest, I am sorrowful,
If apathy be sorrow. I receive
No joy of beauty from this snowflake wool

That wraps so tenderly each writhen tree,
Now that your tenderness is gone from me.
Stark selfishness of sorrow! Yet I grieve.

Stark selfishness of sorrow! Yet I grieve,
Vaguely aware of watchful loves that hold
Their warmth between me and the utter cold.
Patient and generous and wise, they leave
Me here alone with you and grief, yet weave
Sweet walls of roses round us, paly gold,
Soft pink, clear carmine, white, in manifold
Pattern of petals; mossy buds men thieve
From Elfland, high-blown hearts of joy, tall stems
Crowned with great flushes. In our own rose-garden
We are together and I take reproof
From your dear voice that would not have me harden
My soul against such blessing. Love condemns
The sorrow that from love would walk aloof.

The sorrow that from love would walk aloof
Implores forgiveness even while it sins.
One heart is home; the many hearts are inns
With glow of festal joy, with sheltering roof.
Your life was of my life the warp and woof
Whereon most precious friendships, disciplines,
Passions embroidered rich designs. Grief wins
Pardon from love for very love's behoof.
For true love knows that love must still be true,
Not kind pretender nor blind self-deceiver.
It matters not what other mourners do;
I turn that nectar cup I drained with you
Down on the board. No more shall there be Weaver
Of Rainbows in my heaven's too tranquil blue.

No Rainbow Weaver in my heaven's calm blue;
The magic gate through which each common thing
Came shining with a strange transfiguring
Is sealed. Where now shall Grief keep rendez-vous
With Comfort? Nay, I would not learn the new
Who crave the old,—our water from the spring,
Not sacramental wine. The seasons bring
But phantoms of those joys that died with you.
Years pass. The household feasts your old-time guests.
A rose casts shadow on the cloth. Ah, thrust
Of hidden hurt amid the flying jests!
For that dark, silent image to my seeing
Is memory-ghost of your warm, fragrant being.
I could not bear my grief but that I must.

(IV)

Do you remember still your dear-loved earth,
Shadows of stormy clouds that sweep across
Old, castled Heidelberg; the golden gloss
Of sands atoning to the Sphinx for dearth
Of ancient splendors; strange Hawaiian mirth
At arbor feast, where, heedless of their loss,
Their vanishing, those blithe brown folk would toss
Wreathed heads to music, as if life were worth,
Even on such sliding brink, its hour of joy?
Do you remember how the sunsets burned
In Norway skies? Not pain itself could cloy
Your wild-bird heart that ever longed to roam,
That ever for the bluer distance yearned
And on each bough of beauty was at home.

God's bird, upon his every bough at home,
With skylarks on a Devon cliff between
The purple moors and purple sea, in green

Swiss valleys, in fair Florence, royal Rome,
Amid grim totem-poles by frozen foam;
Poplars of France that follow her serene,
Broad rivers; Andalusian groves, with sheen
Of orange and pomegranate, 'neath the dome
Of drowsy convent or above the game
Of choral children; bells of Brittany
Pouring their joyous gloria upon
The villagers, whose piety must don
To please the Saint their quaintest finery.
Horizons flushed about you when you came.

Horizons flushed about you when you came.
Our low skies lifted and the world looked in.
Joy-fellow of the journeying sun and kin
To that wind-god whose feet were plumed with flame,
Still, scholar, teacher, still your steadfast aim
Was understanding of the ways that win
Men upward from a blind, brute origin
To ordered peoples. Ever would you claim
That in our own crude country glows romance
Whereby the elder charm of Europe fades.
Falls of the Rhine you deemed Undine's dance
To great Columbia's thundering cascades.
Prophets that from her cloudy palisades
Summoned the pioneers to glorious chance.

The pioneers who took that glorious chance
You traced o'er plain and mountain, hunters, trappers,
Gold-seekers, prairie schooners with child-nappers
In mother's arms, babes whose inheritance
Of virgin land in limitless expanse
Was won by hero fathers,—daring tappers
Of earth's hid treasuries, unconscious mappers

Of new dominions for mankind's advance.
Their courage beat like joy within your pulse.
Sleeping delicious hours of night away
On a Pacific beach mid shells and dulse.
Children beside you and a young moon beaming
Upon the surf that splashed you in its play,
Even then of their adventure you were dreaming.

Always of their adventure you were dreaming,
Retreading their hard paths and poring long
Over their crabbed scripts, with patience strong
As zest itself, until your mind was teeming
With frontier lore. I laughed to hear it streaming,
Untiring as the red-eyed vireo's song,
From lips folk called reserved nor did them wrong;
But silence had at last its full redeeming.
Your earlier volumes had but blazed the way
For this, your own heart's book, your joy of toil,
To be of all your glad achievement crown.
I watched the gold fruit ripening day by day
And felt your dream's incredulous recoil
When merciless disease would face it down.

Not merciless disease might face it down.
Through those four years beset with wasting pain,
The surgeon's knife again and yet again,
Our spring of joy slow withering to brown
Autumn of ruin, still your dream, like town
Stormed by resistless armies, would not deign
To lower its proud banner. So we twain
Finished your book beneath Death's very frown.
For all the hospital punctilio,
Through the drear night within your mind would grow
Those sentences my morning pen would spring

To meet, while guilty mirth flashed to and fro
From your brave eyes to mine, for joy and woe
As comrades climbed your height of suffering.

Joy climbed with woe your height of suffering.
Oft in your clouded eyes, as if soft-kissed.
Pleasure would brighten, banishing the mist
Of weariness, while from past journeying
Kind memory would many a picture bring,
Your Rockies robed in sunny amethyst,
Or that stupendous canon, annalist
Of all the aeons. To your heart would cling
Sweet, showery Aprils with their miracle
Of leaf and blossom, frozen nature's birth
Into fresh loveliness. Again the spell
Of Italy was on you and you smiled
As when you caught her songs from singing child.
Do you remember still your dear-loved earth?

(V)

Do saints go gypsying in Paradise?
How merrily, escaped from golden street
And jasper wall, your footsteps light and fleet
Would rove the wildwood—wood whose happy spice
And balm conceal no treacherous device
Of trap to snare and shatter small furred feet,
Where no shot bird beats broken wing! Oh, sweet
To taste a joy not bought by sacrifice!
Have you, as on Lake Ripley, bungalow
By water's edge, where from your sunrise bath
To twilight hymn the saucy chipmunks strow
Your floor with shells, scolding in frolic wrath
To see you sweep them forth? And up your path
What other heavenly callers come and go?

What other heavenly callers come and go
To hear your voice, my best of music hushed,
To rest beside the lake on ledges plushed
With moss and watch the tall marsh rushes blow,
Red-shouldered blackbirds flashing to and fro
Above the water-lilies, and the flushed
Breast of the robin guarding nest soft-brushed
By dancing linden leaves? Do cherubs know
Your welcome, as so many children here
Have known it? For you ever used to say
Their joy of laughter was your perfect cure
For weariness. You were so tired. Dear,
Before you died, please God that now with pure
Spirits of childhood you keep holiday.

Spirits of childhood, keeping holiday
On your broad steps that to the rippling lake
Descend, would call on Sigurd to awake
In his low grave. How could our collie stay
With earth, when you had fled so far away?
Our most adoring lover! For love's sake
The seal of death's enchanted door would break,
And Heaven be gladder for his winsome play.
With what a joyful plunge he would chase the stick
Flung forth into that little sea of glass!
How proudly swim with it to shore and flick
A crystal rain on scampering cherubim;
Then, well content, your hand caressing him,
Stretch on the threshold, greeting all who pass.

Over your threshold eagerly would pass
Your blessed dead, on furlough from employ
In that new life where service still is joy,
Parents and sister and the baby lass

Your arms once cherished, now in wisdom's class
So high 'tis hers to train with starry toy
And many a bright, angelical decoy
Your own celestial infancy. The grass
That never withers feels the drawing nigh
Of two dear brothers, yet unused to wend
The ways of Zion, but of instinct true
To find the violet path that leads to you,
And with the later fares a laughing friend
Whom Sigurd springs to meet with lyric cry.

Only for her he lifts his lyric cry,
Lady of Cedar Hill, yet proffers paw
Full cordially to all who, by the law
That brings our own to us at last, though sky
Must melt between, your threshold glorify,
—Our Pearl of Wellesley poets, who would draw
New dreams from Plato; Lincoln, not a flaw
Left on that beauty angels know him by;
Francis the Pitiful, and our vesper bell,
Christina, who while still on earth knew well,
Even as the psalmist king of Israel,
Heaven's joy of harping,—words of hers rose faint
From your pale lips, the last ere silence fell,—
And One with Whom your soul was best acquaint.

That One with Whom your soul was best acquaint,
The wandering Christ Who loved the cedar trees
Of Lebanon, the red anemones
Of Carmel, Whose low bidding put restraint
On stormy waves, Who fled from the complaint
Of hungering multitudes to shores like these,
Reeds shaken with the wind, may He not please
To come to you, His follower. His saint?

Joy of Joys! Beatitude complete!
1 see you kneel to anoint those wayworn feet
With ointment from your alabaster box
Of precious faith. But straightway doubt strikes chilly
Across the heart and my poor babbling mocks.
How may the earth-blind bulb behold the lily?

How may the earth-blind bulb behold the bliss
Of lilies, dance and color, odor, air?
Or iridescent wings their joy declare
To that dark prisoner in the chrysalis?
Thought reels before the metamorphosis
Of mortal to immortal. Lest despair
Rob us of strength for burdens yet to bear,
We tease God's inconceivable with this
Mere childishness of query upon query.
Have they no need of us who need them so?
Do they never, of eternity grown weary,
Long for the river-song of Time's onflow?
Can one tree, even the Tree of Life, suffice?
Do saints go gypsying in Paradise?

(VI)

No more than memory, love's afterglow?
Our quarter century of joy, can it
Be all? The lilting hours like birds would flit
By us, who loitered in the portico
Of love's high palace. Time enough to know
Its court decorum, nor would mind admit
Love's term of learning was not infinite.
Ah, courtesies my carelessness let go!
Then you forsook me ere my love was wise,
Not wise enough to know if still you are,
Too pure a light for my enshadowed eyes,

Or if, unconscious of my very grief.
Your vanished spirit, beautiful as brief.
Be quenched in darkness, like a shooting star.

Quenched in deep darkness, like a shooting star,
Or hidden as the moon within a cloud?
How often have we watched her, silver-browed,
Engulfed by gloom, and soon, upon its far,
Joy-brightened rim, emerge without a scar
On her pale splendor? Do you wear your shroud
So lightly? We but know that disallowed
To mortal vision is your avatar.
Nay, I must journey past all moons, all aid
Of these discarded senses, past all space
And pealing rhythm of time, ere I be made
Spirit to apprehend your spirit face;
Yet of this only is my soul afraid.
That you are merged in some transcendent grace.

If you are merged in some transcendent grace,
Drowned in divinity, ah, then no more
We are ourselves, no longer shall implore
The Power that rushes on its own proud race
Toward terrible perfection at a pace
So passionate that we who would adore
A Father are but bubbles on the roar
Of that tumultuous tide. If such strange case
Be ours, if unappealable decree
Make human love and joy and suffering
A whirl of autumn leaves, heart's mockery,
Speak it, O Science, with authentic voice,
And let us end it now. For who would cling
To such existence, serve such God, by choice?

I choose to serve my hope of God, a hope
Like to the shipwrecked mariner's, whose frail
Boat lurches while he leaps to calk and bail,
Make fast his water-keg with shred of rope,
Still searching, searching, dizzy eyes a-grope,
The blank of ocean for a saving sail.
Not his the fault if whelming seas prevail;
What courage can, he does. So would I cope
With our immensity of doubt, with all
This vast incertitude on which we toss,
Hoping, and striving in the hope I cherish,
Till nought remains to solace or appal.
If hope be truth, 'tis joy. If all be loss,
What matters it to life brought forth to perish?

To life brought forth to perish what is life?
Nought recks the field-mouse peeping from a loop
Of grasses that this evening may bring swoop
Upon him of the owl whose plaintive fife
We echo for our sport. No dread of knife
Troubles those sheep that sedulously droop
Their heads above the clover; even this group
Of calves frisk forth to market without strife.
Wild, pirate hawks cry loud above the caw
Of scandaled citizens, yet hawks and crows
Alike obey commandments that we call
Instinct. In joy the flood of being flows,
Each life the food of higher life, and all
Creatures of earth, sea, air accept the Law.

Why may not we in joy accept the Law?
Is thought a curse that we still chafe in vain,
One blind link more in an unending chain,
Against such doom? We see that children draw

Life from their parents; empires, wisps of straw
On a swift stream, swirl by that man may gain
A firmer basis for a nobler reign;
And yet we would extinction overawe
With our dim spark of God. Oh, what are we,
That in the face of all we witness, still
Clamor and cry for immortality;
Dare to withhold our puny homage till
Some oracle shall tell us if there be
A Will within the Law, and Love that Will?

O Will within the Law, O Love the Will,
To Thee I lift what faltering faith I may,
Longing allegiance fain its vow to pay
In Thy vast temple, but of little skill
To parley with Jehovah. Still, O still
Let her be my interpreter and pray
The prayer I cannot; let as yesterday
Her faith's clear fountain feed my wavering rill.
O yesterday, and all its joy of you!
Just back from morning run, bright locks a-blow
About flushed face, such gladness gleaming through
Candid gray eyes as deepens them to blue,
Arms full of blossoming branches fresh with dew,
You come to memory, love's afterglow.

(VII)

Your sentence by my quavering voice was told.
Amazed, like the forsaken Christ, you viewed
The spectral shape of your appointed rood.
Even as when once autumnal mists unrolled
And gave you, unsuspecting, to behold
For the first time the Alps. Stricken you stood,
Awed, terrified at their bleak magnitude,

And shivered in the sunshine, smitten cold.
But straight you turned, so gallantly that God
Was proud of you, from ways you longed to wend.
From all your joy of life to this new goal,
Resolved to die with honor. Firm of soul,
Wresting a victory from defeat, you trod
Your Via Dolorosa to the end.

Your Via Dolorosa was mine own.
I walked beside you, far as love might go.
I saw, while mortal beauty dimmed, the glow
Of spirit brighten, till the soul had flown,
As birds at some caerulean bidding, known
Only to wings, fly south before the snow
To joy of summer. Left behind, below,
I wait till clouds of time be overblown.
Yet is there not a Way, a Truth, a Life
That my dull, darkened heart may reach you by?
Are not these walls, that watched your passing, rife
With mysteries that on me call and gleam?
Is it no more than pain's importunate dream,
Or do I sometimes feel your presence nigh?

Have I not sometimes felt your presence nigh?
You said: "I will not leave you comfortless,"
And oft half conscious of a swift impress
Upon my spirit, lights that clarify
A problem, calm on storm, ever I try
To hold my listening heart in readiness
For joy of your impalpable caress.
Wisdom of your inaudible reply.
Oh, still shed blessing on me from those wings
Of whose soft tarriance I would be aware,
Light intimations, fleet evanishings,

Speech finer than all syllables, a rare
Shining within my soul, a thrill intense
That breaketh not Death's law of reticence.

It breaketh not Death's law of reticence,
For when I would my miracles declare
They melt as sunset colors in the air
Of evening, and myself oft wonder whence
Came to my heart that brief intelligence
Of a communion eyes and ears forswear
And touch denies. My ebbing joys despair
And charge imagination with pretense.
Is this my lonely camp by love patrolled,
Or am I fooled by credulous desire?
What hand throws balsam on my bivouac fire
When it burns low? Whose is the tender tone
That hushes grief with courage, as of old:
"We will be strong and glad in love alone"?

"We will be strong and glad in love alone."
I can endure through all my desolate days,
But can I share your canticles of praise,
Your adoration at the Great White Throne
That rises for the pure in heart? Can moan
Mount up to singing? How shall summer raise
Beauty from these your ashes? Shall the maize
Ripen in gold where willow-herb was sown?
By seven springs has your far grave been grassed,
And in my depth of sorrow are astir
New powers, perceptions, joys, against my earth
Uppressing, secret agonies of birth.
At bidding of their angel gardener:
"The Life Eternal! Let us hold it fast!"

"Let us hold fast the Life Eternal!" So
You bade me, so I strive, a better lover
Than I shall be a saint. Oh, starspace rover,
Would we might stroll once more, as long ago,
Startling the bobolinks, across the glow
Of Wellesley meadows lit by yellow clover
With "God in all," you murmured, and "God over
All beauty and all joy"! For as I know
Your soul enfolding mine, you dwelt in Him,
Dwelt in the Light of God, How clearly fall
On memory your words, when once your breath
Waited the ether, and my eyes went dim!
"Oh, have no fear, Dear Heart, for life and death
Are one," you smiled, "and God is All in All,"

Forevermore is God your All in All.
In His eternal radiance you dwell,
Fulfilling His High Word as sunbeams quell
These earthly shadows. In your dying, gall
You tasted, felt the spear your flesh appal,
Were crucified with Christ, but it is well
With you at last in that bright citadel
Pain cannot storm, beyond the shining wall
Grief may not scale. That terror of all men,
The gate of gloom, is now your gate of gold.
Sore-tested, your heroic heart has won
The pearl of peace. More quietly than when
Your sentence by my quavering voice was told,
I give you joy, my Dearest. Death is done.

Acknowledgments

On May 17, 2018, we had a "surfboard" party, a chance to thank the friends and family who keep us above water, of which there are so many. It would be impossible to thank everyone who has been kind along this journey; to our surfboard, please know that I cherish your friendship and I am so grateful that you kept the girls and me afloat.

Sophie, Liv, and Bliss: I am so sorry you had to endure this loss so early in your lives, but I am so incredibly proud of the people you are, forged out of your heart and your experiences. I am grateful that from the beginning you let Tommy first into my life, and then opened yourselves to his love. I could not be prouder of how you have grieved him so well, and with so much love. I am forever indebted to your kindness to me. You seemed to have learned early that life is for the living, and your curiosity and bravery in the world are inspiring. Sophie, thank you especially for reading along with my writing, I am inspired by the traveler, writer, and woman you are becoming. Liv, I am proud that after taking care of us, you knew how to take care of yourself, taking a gap year to renew yourself, find your purpose and set off on your path. Bliss, you and I are here still, in the Scarab, keeping our love alive and our lives moving forward. You have grown the most over the past three years, while always staying true to your loyal, loving self. We all know how proud Tommy was of each of you; just imagine what he would say now! I love you.

Considering the all-encompassing support they are in my life, my family is grossly underrepresented in this narrative. Their love is my foundation, and so it seems like it became the backdrop. Mom, Dad, Chrissie, John, Jimmy, Debbie, Sam, Matt, Nicolas, Lucie, Charlie, Phoebe, and the Hoveland, Lawrence, and Burgoyne clans: We are so lucky to have each other. Special thanks to Jonathan for adopting me as your big sis, and showing me how to get on your bike every damn day (for four years and counting). Thank you for getting me, and us, through this time and everything else, I love you.

Thank you to all of Tommy's friends and family who have adopted us into your lives. You all knew and loved Tommy way longer than I did, and

I can only imagine that reading this version of my story of him might be strange given the arc and depth of your relationships. For Aaron, Ben, and Caleb, you were the most important of all humans to your dad, first, last, and always, and we are grateful that you shared your father with us. For Peter, Nancy, Margi, Brien, Connie, Kevin, Mary Jane, and John, thank you for bringing us into your fold. Our world got bigger and richer for the love of the Coluccis and Robustellis. Andrew and Jeannette; Chris and Bridget, thank you for watching out for me in Tommy's stead. I know you know what that would mean to him.

Karen and Robbie Brewer, Joe and Karen Brooks, Doug Fitzgerald, Edie and Sam Goethal, Chris Kelly, Nancy Keyes, Christine Netski, Eamon O'Marah, Jennifer Sleeper, Fernando Tavares, Paul Gorman, Mary Orne, and the Quincey Y crew: I have loved getting to know Tommy better through you, and becoming new friends—thank you.

My friends have been my backbone. Many of you appear in the story, others of you read every line, and you all inspired every ounce of healing: Emily Abedon, Dave Ackerman and Anna Towns, Beth Baker, Caroline Bagby, Henry Blodget, Jamie Blosser, Dana Bourland, Debbie Briggs, Angie Brooks and Larry Scarpa, Mike and Karen Buckley, Bob and Amee Burgoyne, Steven Burks, Sarah Butter, John Cary, Johnny Cator and Stephanie Crote, Catherine Clark, Harry Connolly, Emily Coombs, Kim Cory, April DeSimone, Karen Devito, Maura Dolan, Lynn Donahue, Christina Dougherty, Lisa and Oliver Dow, Kimberlee Dowdell, Jeana Dunlap, Maria Enos, Brad Feldman and Liz Graham, Washington Fajardo, Alice T. Friedman, Lucilla Fuller Marvel, Kim Giangrasso, Rachel Gleeson, Jeanne and Brooks Goddard, Jeannie Goldstone, Kira Gould, Lesedi Graveline, Aleita Hall, Stephanie Hawkinson, Sandra Higgins, Theo Hill, Claudia Hinz, Matt Hoffman, Sara Just, David Kazanjian, Lisa Keeler, Michael Smith Masis, Martha McNamara, Annie Newman, Kathryn Rogers Merlino, David Mistretta, Mary Beth Mohan, Lindsey Mullen, Dan Murphy, Michael Murphy, Lisa and Brad Neighbors, Marc Norman, Siobhan O'Riordan, Dave and Meagan Occhialini, Jennie Lister Oldfield, Betsy Peyton, Jenny Rademacher, Rob Reynolds, Alan Ricks, Judi Rizley, David Rowe, Karston Robbins, Emma Russell, Amy Salvucci,

Robin Saunders, Ben Schonzeit, Sue Ann Sheehan, Holly Sorensen, Jessica Teperow, Mayrah Udvardi, Vilma Verissimo, Kirby Vernon, Jonathan Walton, and Walker Wells.

I also have to thank Wellesley High School, all the teachers, and coaches who supported us so beautifully. To the parent community—especially the hockey parents—we love being your family! And to all the friends and teammates of Sophie, Liv and Bliss, nothing could be more amazing than to have at least 50 of you in our front hall on May 17, 2017. Thank you for being so supportive to each of the girls, and to all of us.

I give special thanks to my yoga community at HYP Studios, especially Jordan Lashley, Braxton Rose, and Tara Morris. Tara, you are my sister now; thank you for your unquenchable thirst for living life with as much courage and love as possible.

I am so grateful that this book itself is a work of art. Nicole Vecchiotti encouraged me on the path to publishing, and Kristin Von Ogtrop introduced me to Sarah Humphries Collins, who helped me edit. Rebecca Bakken has been my copy editor, throughout the writing. Sophie, Liv, and Bliss read from Courtney L. Martin and Wendy MacNaughton's illustrated manifesto at Tommy's funeral, and it is the most inspired way to start this book. Thank you to Tommy Schapperkotter for drawing the Scarab. Thank you for your beautiful photographs, Harry Connolly, and for your support through the writing process. Thank you to Zoe Miller for your magical illustrations on the cover and throughout. Thank you to Amy Wilkins and Robin Brunelle at Matsumoto Incorporated for bringing all this love and creativity together in a gorgeous book design. For Cheryl Weber at Schiffer Publishing, what can I say? Two books at one time? You have been at my side for two years and never lost faith. Thank you for giving me this chance to uphold my wedding vow to Tommy.

Thanks to the Wellesley Historical Society, Wellesley College Archives, and the Trust for Public Land for help with research and photo documentation. Enterprise Community Partners and the Enterprise Rose Fellows have been my work family. Special thanks to Terri Ludwig and Laurel Blatchford, as well as Kate Deans, Ray Demers, Carrie Niemy, Meghan Venable-Thomas, and Nella Young, who kept the boat afloat while I was sinking, and to every single Rose Fellow, with special thanks to James Arentson, who sent me ♥ every single day for a year. The opportunity to be a Loeb Fellow at the Graduate School of Design at Harvard University allowed me to reintegrate myself during year two, understanding how love and kindness are also a design approach to the world. That time and space allowed me to reintegrate my personal and professional selves, resulting in *Design with Love: At Home in America*, a publication in partnership with Harry Connolly and also by Schiffer Publishing, another book about love and home, but this time told through the Rose Fellowship communities. And to my new work family, MASS Design Group, I am so grateful to be working with each of you to research, build and advocate for architecture that promotes justice and human dignity.

And, lastly, to the Katharines—the Katies, Ms. Bates and Ms. Coman: Thank you for envisioning and building this glorious house, the Scarab, and for reserving a special room within it, Bohemia. Thank you for sharing your home, your love, your grief, and your poetry with me. I am glad to now share them with others.

For Further Reading

Abrams, Douglas Carlton, Desmond Tutu, and Dalai Lama. *The Book of Joy: Lasting Happiness in a Changing World*. New York: Avery, 2016.

Alexander, Elizabeth. *The Light of the World*. New York: Grand Central Publishing, 2015.

Bates, Katherine Lee. *Selected Poems of Katharine Lee Bates*. Edited by Marion Pelton Guild. Boston: Houghton Mifflin, 1930.

Bates, Katharine Lee. *Yellow Clover*. New York: E. P. Dutton, 1922.

Brown, Abbie Farwell. *Round Robin*. New York: E. P. Dutton, 1921.

Burgess, Dorothy. *Dream and Deed: The Story of Katharine Lee Bates*. Norman: University of Oklahoma Press, 1952.

Coman, Katharine. *The Industrial History of the United States*. New York: Macmillan, 1912.

Compton's Pictured Encyclopedia. 8 vols. Chicago: F. E. Compton, 1922.

Cortázar, Julio. *Hopscotch*. Translated by Gregory Rabassa. New York: Pantheon Books, 1966.

Didion, Joan. *The Year of Magical Thinking*. New York: Vintage Books, 2007.

Friedman, Alice. "Hiding in Plain Site: Love, Life and the Queering of Domesticity in Early Twentieth-Century New England." *Home Cultures* 12, no. 2 (4 May 2015): 1–28.

Gawande, Atul. *Being Mortal: Medicine and What Matters in the End*. New York: Henry Holt, 2014.

Goldman, Francisco. *Say Her Name.* New York: Grove, 2011.

Hawthorne, Nathaniel. *The House of Seven Gables: A Romance.* Introduction by Katharine Lee Bates. New York: Thomas Y. Crowell, 1902.

Hickman, Martha Whitmore. *Healing after Loss: Daily Meditations for Working through Grief.* New York: Harper Collins, 1994.

Kalanithi, Paul. *When Breath Becomes Air.* New York: Random House, 2016.

Leopold, Ellen. *My Soul is among Lions: Pages from the Breast Cancer Archives.* Charleston, SC: Valley Green, 2013.

Magnusson, Margareta. *The Gentle Art of Swedish Death Cleaning: How to Free Yourself and Your Family from a Lifetime of Clutter.* New York: Scribner, 2018.

Mann, Dorothea Lawrence. *Katharine Lee Bates: Poet and Professor.* Boston: Dorothea Lawrence Mann, 1931.

Marvel, Lucilla Fuller. *Listen to What They Say.* San Juan: La Editorial, Universidad de Puerto Rico, 2008.

McFarland, Philip. *Hawthorne in Concord.* New York: Grove, 2004.

Oliver, Mary. *A Thousand Mornings: Poems.* New York: Penguin Books, 2012.

Ponder, Melinda M. *Katharine Lee Bates: From Sea to Shining Sea.* Chicago: Windy City, 2017.

Richardson, Robert D., Jr. *Emerson: The Mind on Fire.* Berkeley: University of California Press, 1995.

Rinpoche, Sogyal. *The Tibetan Book of Living and Dying*. San Francisco: HarperCollins, 1992.

Sandberg, Sheryl, and Adam Grant. *Option B: Facing Adversity, Building Resilience, and Finding Joy*. New York: Alfred A. Knopf, 2017.

Sherr, Lynn. *America the Beautiful: The Stirring True Story behind Our Nation's Favorite Song*. New York: Public Affairs, 2001.

Strayed, Cheryl. *Tiny Beautiful Things: Advice on Love and Life from Dear Sugar*. New York: Vintage Books, 2012.

Wheeler, Brownell H. *One Life, Many Deaths: A Surgeon's Stories*. Cambridge, MA: Meredith Winter, 2014.

Wineapple, Brenda. *Hawthorne: A Life*. New York: Random House, 2004.